Erik H. Erikson
Explorer of Identity and the Life Cycle

Other titles in Mind Shapers Series

Forthcoming titles in Mind Shapers Series

Also by Richard Stevens

Erik H. erikson

explorer of identity and the life cycle

Richard Stevens

Mind Shapers – Key Psychologists and their impact
Series Editor: Richard Stevens

palgrave
macmillan

Revised Edition of *Erik Erikson: An Introduction*, Open University Press, 1983

First published 2008 by
PALGRAVE MACMILLAN
Houndmills, Basingstoke, Hampshire RG21 6XS and
175 Fifth Avenue, New York, N.Y. 10010
Companies and representatives throughout the world

PALGRAVE MACMILLAN is the global academic imprint of the Palgrave Macmillan division of St. Martin's Press, LLC and of Palgrave Macmillan Ltd. Macmillan® is a registered trademark in the United States, United Kingdom and other countries. Palgrave is a registered trademark in the European Union and other countries.

ISBN 13: 978–1–4039–9986–3
ISBN 10: 0–1–4039–9986–3

This book is printed on paper suitable for recycling and made from fully managed and sustained forest sources. Logging, pulping and manufacturing processes are expected to conform to the environmental regulations of the country of origin.

A catalogue record for this book is available from the British Library.

A catalogue record for this book is available from the Library of Congress.

10   9   8   7   6   5   4   3   2   1
17   16   15   14   13   12   11   10   09   08

Printed in China

Contents

Personal Acknowledgements

I would like to express my appreciation of Erik Erikson for the stimulation of his ideas and for being such a warm and forthcoming person to interview. Without the persuasion of Dr Olga Coschug-Toates this book would never have been written. My warm thanks also to my fellow writer Dr Annette Thomson for her comments on chapters, and providing constant encouragement and stimulating discussion; to my colleague Jane Henry who gave me perceptive comments; and to Nevia Frleta who offered not only emotional sustenance but also the use of her sky room in which some of this book was written. I want to thank also my PA Elaine de Bastos for her unswerving and comforting assistance throughout the project.

Thanks too to my editors – Jaime Marshall and especially Anna Van Boxel and Neha Sharma for their continued support for this book and the *Mindshapers* series. Shirley Tan our copyeditor provided calm and impeccable professional backup. Finally my gratitude to Andrew McAleer for his enthusiasm and hard work in getting this project under way.

1 Introducing Erik H. Erikson

Many years ago, when I was a young lecturer at Trinity College, Dublin, my then Head of Department asked me to review a book for a staff and postgraduate seminar group. The book was *Childhood and Society*. It was my first introduction to the writings of Erik Erikson. I have to confess that there were moments in my initial reading of the first chapters when I put the book down to reflect on whether this was just a lot of awkward verbiage. Or were there hidden in the words ideas that illuminated our understanding of human behaviour? I persevered and, as I progressed further into this rich and complex book, I began to appreciate the wisdom and insights into the human condition which reading Erikson offers.

Though the response to his work by other analysts has sometimes been muted, many are in no doubt about his importance. Elizabeth Mayer describes him as 'one of the most extraordinary psychoanalysts our field has seen'.[1] Seligman and Shanok write of 'Erikson's unique and profound vision'.[2] Roazen accepts that Erikson is acknowledged as one of the foremost psychologist of our time' and argues that he revitalized the Freudian tradition.[3] There is certainly no doubt about the enthusiasm of the general intellectual public. The historian Friedman describes him as 'a major influence in American intellectual life… perhaps the most significant post-Freudian thinker'.[4] The poet W.H. Auden commented on a book of Erikson's that it was 'so full of wise observations about human life that no quotations could it justice'.[5] Statesmen also acknowledged him – Al Gore was one of Erikson's students and Bill Clinton an admirer.

If I open this book with such laudatory references, it is to demonstrate that I am not the only one to find great value in Erikson's work. And when we remember that his focus is on people's personal lives – their development through life, their sense of identity and their relationship with society, his insights into these topics have personal and social relevance today. They make Erikson an ideal subject for this *Mindshapers* series on thinkers who help to shape our understanding of the human condition. But what Erikson offers is not pat prescriptions or packaged formulae but what in his own words he describes as 'tools to think with'. As Welchman comments, 'when faced with some particularly confusing or intractable question, I could often find in returning to Erikson's writings, if not an answer, at least an insight, a thought-provoking response or a path to follow'.[6]

However, if others value his work as much as I, many also find Erikson's work not always easily assimilable. Reading Erikson has been described as 'like walking in a dense and beautiful forest with a thousand paths leading through it'.[7] In such a situation you require a guide; and that is what this book aims to provide.

Erikson's writings are diverse – often in the form of essays or collections of essays. They sprawl. It takes time to grasp their essence and the very real understanding they provide. My purpose in this book is to try to capture and communicate that more straightforwardly. So that the reader will by the end have a clear vision of the core ideas in Erikson's writing and begin to appreciate the deep insights he contributes. He has certainly profoundly influenced my own thinking about psychological issues. If this book can convey, as I hope it does, something of the essence and freshness of Erikson's approach and, in particular, stimulates the reader to look at Erikson's own writings (for which this book provides a map), then it will have served its purpose well. Erikson has much to say about both personality and society that is highly relevant in the contemporary world and I will focus on this in the final chapter.

Erikson is important not only for the very considerable influence he has had in disseminating psychoanalytic ideas but also because his work embodies key developments in psychoanalytic thought since Freud. He has roots in both the old world of psychoanalysis and the new. As a young man, he was a frequent visitor to Sigmund Freud's house. He was analysed by Freud's daughter Anna and made the acquaintance of several of the original members of the psychoanalytic movement. But in 1933 he joined the many analysts who emigrated from an increasingly tense Europe to seek a new future in the USA. He not only experienced life in a different culture and learned to practise there as an analyst, but he also worked as an academic and researcher, with both anthropologists and psychologists as close colleagues.

With Erich Fromm[8] and Karen Horney, he is usually described as a neo-Freudian (though he preferred the term 'post-Freudian'). All three were emigrés and, because of this experience, they were particularly sensitized to the profound effects of the culture in which a person lives. One key thrust of Erikson's work is to explore the complex relationship between social context and individual development, particularly as this is mediated through styles of child-rearing. Like many other analysts since Freud, Erikson also places greater emphasis on the ego – that part of personality concerned with directing action, coping with the external world and integrating competing urges within the self. His particular focus here has been on the healthy ego – how this develops and how it is maintained. Whereas Freud's conceptualization of development largely stopped at puberty, Erikson is concerned to trace the evolution of the ego throughout life.

While extending psychoanalytic thought in these ways, Erikson nevertheless remains within the essential spirit of Freud's approach. His particular strength is to bring psychoanalytic concepts alive. His vivid case analyses show psychoanalysis in action at its best. But, with his interest in conscious experience, the relation between the individual and society, and psychological development not just in childhood but throughout life, there is also a humanistic quality about his work. His concern is with the fundamental human condition – how can we make sense of our lives and best forge the trajectory of our futures? In this respect his writings often seem to carry the potential to increase whatever store of human wisdom the reader may possess.

A sense of coherence and evolution marks the pattern of Erikson's writings. Ideas planted initially almost as asides come to full flower in books and papers years later. Like a person developing, each stage of his work builds on the previous ones. They unfold from each other and reflect his changing experiences. His approach is characterized by a healthy respect for the richness and complexity of human life. He refuses the temptations to simplify or over-formalize his conceptions. With a few exceptions, these tend to emerge from working analyses, rather than being set out in schematic form. For these reasons, his ideas are not always easy to pin down. People who may have heard of his theories quite often know very little of what they contain. It is the primary purpose of this book to rectify this by presenting his ideas concisely and lucidly in the context of the developing cycle of his work.

Erikson is best known for his conceptions of *identity* and the *life cycle*. He emphasizes the importance of the study of identity to our time. Whereas for Freud's patients the key issue was sexuality and the repressions that social life demanded, for people in the contemporary Western world at least, it becomes the problem of creating who they are and the persons they may become. In his concept of the life cycle Erikson traces ego development from early childhood through maturity to old age by exploring the ego qualities which emerge and are crucial to each stage.

One theme which, though less in evidence, runs throughout his work, is his emphasis on *integration*. To understand any individual, we need to see him or her both as a biological and social being. Freud realized the significance of this interface – that the human person is at once physical and symbolic, and is caught between the interplay of drives and of meanings. But he failed fully to confront the difficulties – both for method and theory – which this Janus face of humankind gives rise to. Erikson at least tries to deal with it directly. In several case studies, he analyses actions and experiences specifically in terms of the interactions between the biological basis and social context in which each occurs and its significance in the experience and development of the individuals concerned.

Erikson's background in psychoanalysis alerts him to the constructed nature of any theory or analysis – in other words, that it rests on assumptions which themselves require to be made explicit. In his vivid case studies, particularly his detailed historical portraits of Luther and Gandhi, he does not shy at reflecting on the possible biases which might underlie his own analyses. He draws our attention to the intrinsic limitations of psychobiography and the formidable methodological problems posed by *any* attempt to encapsulate the life and character of another human being.

Each of these major themes will be dealt with in turn as they emerge in the evolution of Erikson's thought. While some critical comment will be offered as the book proceeds, the emphasis will be on conveying the essence of his ideas. Substantive evaluation of his overall contribution will be left until the concluding chapter.

As indicated, Erikson's work often seems to spring from his personal experience. So, to set the scene, the book begins with a brief sketch of the pattern of his life. This will be taken up again in the final chapter where links will be drawn between specific aspects of his life and work.

Erikson's writings presume acceptance of certain basic psychoanalytic ideas. He takes for granted, for example, the significance of the unconscious and the ways it can influence our dreams, fantasies, actions and what we say.

He accepts that the sequence of early experience, particularly in relation to psychosexual development, will play a crucial role in determining later personality. Reading this account of Erikson's work, nevertheless, should demand no more of the reader than the very basic familiarity with psychoanalysis that is part of the common currency of our culture. Should you feel the need though for a substantial and readable grounding in the psychoanalytic tradition from which Erikson emerged, you might like to look at another title in the *Mindshapers* series – *Sigmund Freud: Examining the Essence of his Contribution*.[9]

Erik H. Erikson © Ted Streshinsky/CORBIS

2 A Brief Biography

Perhaps not surprisingly for the man for whom identity would become the core issue, the origins of Erikson's own sense of self were complex. His very attractive mother Karla Abrahamsen was Danish and from a comfortably-off, middle class, Jewish family. She had parted with her first husband on their honeymoon in Rome. He vanished abroad and she never saw him again. When Karla became pregnant a few years later, she was sent to live with some aunts in Germany where in 1902 Erik was born. For appearance's sake, her absent husband was declared to be his father, although they had parted long before Erik could have been conceived. Erikson was never to know who his biological father was. His mother would never tell him and this subsequently became the source of some friction between them. All that Erikson could discover later from other relatives was that his father was probably Danish, gentile and possibly an artist. He fantasized that he might have been a Danish aristocrat and that he had been named after him.

For the first three years of his life, Erik had no competitor for his mother's affections. Then, after her first husband had been declared dead, Karla remarried. Her second husband was a Jewish paediatrician from Karlsruhe, the German town in which they lived. The newly-weds took little Erik on their honeymoon boat trip to Copenhagen. As his new stepfather wanted to be accepted as Erik's real father, the boy's surname was changed from Salomonsen (the name of his mother's first husband) to his own – Homburger. Erikson reported later that he was old enough to sense this 'loving deceit' and, while his new father was caring enough, he felt this might have served to undermine yet further a firm sense of his own identity. As he grew older, further issues arose. Because he was tall, blonde and blue-eyed, he stood out at the synagogue as different. At the local school, the converse applied, he was different because he was known to be Jewish. While accepting the German nationality of his birth, he maintained strong links with his mother's family in Denmark through frequent visits. Thus he felt both Jew and Gentile, German and Danish and yet not fully identified with any of these. While being brought up in a strictly practising Jewish family, he distanced himself from such orthodoxy. As an adolescent, he became fascinated with Christianity, which he encountered through the family of friends. He was particularly close to a schoolmate who graduated in his year (and who was to figure significantly in his life) – Peter Blos. Peter's father Edwin introduced Erik not only to Goethe's ideas, but also to Gorky and Gandhi, both of whom were to figure prominently in his later writings.

At school, Erik's primary interests had been in history, languages and art and he went on to enter the local art school. In 1922 he moved to Munich where he studied art for a further two years. This was interspersed with taking time out – walking in the Black Forest and staying near Lake Constance, sketching and writing his thoughts and reflections. He then moved on to Italy, settling for a time in Florence. These wanderings, made possible by his mother's support, he later ascribed to his own prolonged search for a coherent identity.

Eventually, at the age of 25, he arrived in Vienna where Peter Blos had invited him to help run a small school whose aim was to develop new and creative teaching methods. This marked the beginning of the most significant period in his life. He immediately took to teaching. Although some of his students commented later on his awkward, slightly anxious manner, he connected intuitively with them and enjoyed the close emotional connections with children which the experimental Hietzing school allowed. Sigmund Freud's daughter Anna had begun to practice analysis with children and many of the pupils in the school were her patients or had parents who were either being analysed or were psychoanalysts themselves. Erikson was drawn into their circle and eventually underwent a training analysis with Anna Freud. As part of his training, he did therapeutic work with adolescents and adults as well as children. He also became a regular attender at the intimate and intensive seminars held by the Vienna Psychoanalytic Society, often in the homes of members. In this way he came into close contact with the group around Freud. He met Wilhelm Reich, for example, who eventually split from Freud to follow his own ideas about the repression of sexuality by society and to develop his 'orgone' therapy. In several cases, we can see seeds sown that were later to flower in Erikson's own work. Erik was supervised in his theoretical studies by analysts such as Heinz Hartmann and Paul Federn, who emphasized

the importance of ego development – a key theme in his own subsequent work. Anna too was working on a book on ego defence mechanisms.
Erik also got to know August Aichhorn who was doing pioneering
analytic work with adolescents. Erik also made the acquaintance of Freud
himself. They would see each other occasionally at Freud's house where
Erikson went for his analytic sessions and sometimes also at social events.
It seems though that they conversed little. Erikson was inhibited by shyness
and diffidence and Freud by the pain which speaking caused him for, by
that time, he was in his early seventies and had undergone surgery for
cancer of his jaw.

Erik's relationship with Anna Freud was marked by ambivalence. On the
one hand, he was flattered by her invitation to become her analysand. She
also opened doors for him and through her he met with some of the most
significant figures in psychoanalysis, including of course Freud himself.
On the other, he felt somewhat isolated as one of Anna's only few male
analysands. The fact that she also analysed some of the students at his
school as well as himself could not have helped matters. By today's stan-
dards, it was certainly a rather unorthodox arrangement. They saw each
other socially outside the sessions. Erik even reports that she did her knit-
ting on occasion during their sessions (once presenting him with a sweater
for his baby son). Anna Freud shared a waiting room with her father. Before
his sessions Erik would often see Freud opening the door to his consulting
room to let in his next patient. This set Erik wondering if he should not
have been analysed by the founder of psychoanalysis himself. His training seminars were also dominated by experienced older women analysts
(his 'aunt-ensemble' as he later called them) who both intimidated him
and led him to marvel at the quality of their insights.

Erikson stayed in Vienna for six years. During this time he studied the
methods of Montessori education, as well as teaching at the school and
continuing to paint. He also took a variety of courses at the University of
Vienna in subjects that interested him such as education and medicine
though he did not complete any formal qualification. Then in 1929, he
met a Canadian girl he had met at a fancy-dress ball. Joan Serson was a
student of dance. They soon moved into the same house and the following year, after she became pregnant, they got married. Joan was to provide
a strong and invaluable emotional base for Erik throughout his life.

In 1933 at the age of 31 Erik was voted into the Vienna Psychoanalytic
Society as a full member. Although the somewhat unorthodox papers he

first submitted had been regarded with a degree of suspicion by senior analysts, he was appreciated for his creativity and the success of his work with children: also, of course, for his strong connections with the Freud family. This membership meant he could practice as an analyst anywhere in the world. At about this time, the Nazis had begun to burn Freud's books in Berlin and were threatening Austria. Several analysts had already left to seek a future abroad. With their two young sons, Erik and Joan Homburger joined the exodus. Their initial move was to Copenhagen. Even with the full support of his relatives, however, Erik was unsuccessful in his attempt to gain Danish nationality and permission to work there. Psychoanalysis was not popular with the medical authorities in Denmark at the time. So, after six months there, the Homburger family took a boat for America.

On their arrival in the USA, several old friends, including Peter Blos and another old school friend, who were already living there, helped the Homburger family to settle in. They provided introductions to influential contacts who were to serve Erik well. His mother-in-law, who had arranged their visas, also set up housing for them in Boston and supported them until Erik could earn money. He found that America lived up to its reputation as the land of opportunity. As a member of the International Psychoanalytic Association, he was welcomed into the American Association in spite of his lack of medical qualifications, a privilege which was to become increasingly rare. After brief spells in New York and Philadelphia, he began practising as an analyst in the Boston area, working primarily with children and soon gained a reputation for his intuitive insights and effectiveness. He was invited to do research with the Harvard Psychological Clinic. He toyed with the idea of taking a graduate degree in psychology there himself but soon abandoned this. What was important about this time for him was the widening of his intellectual horizons. He not only worked with children of the wealthy but also with the poor he saw at the clinic. He observed, listened to and talked with students. He began to use the English he had practised on the Atlantic crossing and in small seminars exchanged ideas with others from different disciplines. He came into close contact not just with eminent psychologists like Henry Murray and Kurt Lewin but subsequently also with anthropologists such as Gregory Bateson, Ruth Benedict and, in particular, Margaret Mead. This refusal to remain immersed in a psychoanalytic coterie set a pattern which was to run throughout his work. It provided an important source of his conceptual breadth and his appreciation of the assumptions on which his own psychoanalytic orientation depended. These contacts also provided an important source of stimulation for the development of his own ideas.

Three years after his arrival in America, he was offered a full-time teaching and research appointment based at Yale University. All did not run entirely smoothly and his individualistic approach was often at odds with the scientific and co-operative working style of his American colleagues. Then in the summer of 1937 he made a trip that was to prove a significant landmark in the development of his thinking about the relationship between individuals and their culture. With the guidance of the anthropologist Scudder Mekeel he visited a Sioux Indian Reservation in Dakota. (Interestingly, Erik's relationship with Mekeel had been cemented in Boston by his successful treatment of his daughter. His effectiveness in treating children also helped with several other influential contacts, such as John Dollard, a key member of the Institute of Human Relations at Yale).

Most of the rest of Erik's life was to be spent in the USA, divided between stays on East and West Coasts, with brief trips to Europe, Mexico and India. Erik's professional career was beginning to develop well and in 1938 he applied for and was granted American citizenship. He decided to use the occasion to change his name. Although this practice was common among Jewish emigrés to circumvent anti-Semitism; given the origins of his own name, for Erik this was perhaps a way of consolidating his identity. With the full support of his family, the surname chosen was Erikson, though he kept Homburger as his middle name.

In that year, however, family matters became more problematic. His younger son Jon developed a serious illness which happened to coincide with the birth of his daughter Sue. Erik, who to Joan's distress rarely took much of a direct role in bringing up the children, was away observing the Sioux for much of this time. There were worries too over the family he had left behind in Germany. With the rise of the Nazis, his mother and stepfather left for Palestine, as did his stepsisters. Erik sent money to help them to survive.

The following year, the Eriksons moved to California. Through personal contacts Erik had received an invitation to join the Institute of Child Welfare at the University of California at Berkeley. Here, he worked with a team engaged in a longitudinal study of child development. This involved studying 200 normal children aged 11 to 13 with the goal of facilitating adjustment to adolescence. Erik's lack of experience of research methods and his usual difficulty with team research again eventually led to dissatisfaction on both sides. After three years, he agreed to go half-time. This posed little problem for him as he was able to increase his income by taking on more private clients.

The Eriksons spent another ten years in California. In addition to his research and work as a child and training analyst, Erik also helped with wartime projects. One, for example, was to analyse German propaganda including Hitler's speeches; another was to study psychological aspects of life in submarines. Towards the end of the war he also served as a consultant advising on the psychiatric treatment of battle veterans. During his time in California, Erikson made the effort to deepen his knowledge of history and anthropology both of which were to yield rich dividends in his later work. The anthropologist Alfred Kroeber gave him the opportunity to complement his observations of the Sioux. Together they made a field trip to Northern California to see and talk with the Yurok Indians.

Family problems intensified with the birth in 1944 of a Down's syndrome child they named Neil. The Eriksons followed the advice of their medical advisers and agreed to remove Neil to a special clinic. The other children were given to believe that their baby brother had died at birth. Not until seven years had elapsed, did the two youngest learn the truth. Neil was never publicly acknowledged by Erikson. Most neighbours and colleagues assumed that the child psychoanalyst had a happy family of three children only. However, the situation put a considerable strain on the relationship between Joan and Erik and at several points they contemplated divorce. It is intriguing to think what might have become of Erik without Joan, for he depended completely on her, not only for running the family, organizing domestic affairs, but for his own clothing and food. She also edited, advised and sometimes rewrote sections of his work. Erik and Joan were in Italy some 20 years later when Neil died, and it was left to his siblings Jon and Sue to bury him.

Eventually, in 1949, Erikson was offered a professorship at the University of California. It proved short-lived however. Along with all other members of faculty, he was required to sign a mandatory oath of loyalty dissociating himself from groups and individuals affiliated with the Communist Party. In company with several other academics, he refused to do this on principle even though he made clear that he was not a communist. Though he resigned his professorship he nevertheless continued to work at the university for another year.

Erikson's years in California gave him many opportunities to study closely the behaviours of both children and adults. By this time, he had published several journal articles, including clinical case histories and accounts of his use of play therapy with children. His aim now was to gather these together in a book pivoted on the related themes of child development and the relationship of personality to society. This became his first book, *Childhood and Society,* which was published in 1950. As we shall see in the next chapter, this book contains many of his key ideas. They were derived not only from his psychoanalytic work with adults and children but also from his anthropological observations.

In 1951, again with the help of personal contacts, Erikson was offered an appointment at the Austen Riggs Center in Stockbridge, Massachusetts. It was an attractive position with a clinic specializing in psychoanalytic training and research. It included a substantial salary, time for clinical work and writing and a related professorship at the University of Pittsburgh. It proved an agreeable time for Erikson. He enjoyed the beautiful small town where they lived and the intellectual and social contacts that the area provided. The clinic was run on open lines and many of the patients were adolescents. Erikson's teenage daughter was the only child to move with her parents to Stockbridge. His two sons by now were at college. It is perhaps not surprising that Erikson's thoughts began to turn to the problems confronted by young people and, in particular, the question of identity. His work was beginning to attract wider attention. The broad and interdisciplinary nature of Erikson's ideas interested biologists, historians and theologians as well as other psychoanalysts. His own ideas were departing from the emphasis on instinct in psychoanalytic orthodoxy to place stress much more on identity and ego involvement. So he felt particularly honoured to be invited (along with his mentor from his Vienna days – Heinz Hartmann) to the University of Frankfurt – the town of his birth, to speak in celebration of the centenary anniversary of Freud's birth. He also visited Geneva to exchange ideas at a World Health Organization conference with, among others, Jean Piaget, Julian Huxley and Konrad Lorenz.

In 1960, in spite of the fact that he still had no degree, he was appointed Professor of Human Development and Lecturer in Psychiatry at Harvard. Given his lack of credentials this was a somewhat controversial appointment but he had influential allies. At Harvard his teaching focused on his notions of the cycle of psychological development throughout life. He brought in guest lecturers such as Benjamin Spock, Margaret Mead and even the hippie poet Allen Ginsberg. He was greatly helped by a team of graduate assistant teachers, many of whom went on to become distinguished psychologists themselves. He also had students who were later to become famous including the future US Vice President Al Gore.

He continued to visit abroad, giving a talk at the Royal Society in London in 1965. In particular, during the early sixties, he spent some time in India. Although he was fascinated by India, he lived in luxury in the home of Indian friends of friends and hardly experienced the reality of life for most Indian people. But from his experience there grew his psychobiographical study of Gandhi.

He retired from Harvard in 1970 and moved back to Stockbridge, but spent the summers at another house they had bought on the coast. By this time, Erikson had become something of a cultural hero. He had received two invitations to the White House (from Presidents Johnson and Nixon). He was awarded honorary doctorates from Yale and Berkeley as well as other universities and was appointed to the first Freud Memorial Chair at University College London. In 1970 he appeared on the front page of the New York Times magazine described as the 'most influential of living psychoanalysts'.

In 1973 he moved with Joan to California to live in Belvedere and later in Tiburon – across the bay from San Francisco where he continued to write and develop his ideas. Although he was rated as one of the five most cited authors in psychology, appreciation of his work became more mixed and he was dismayed to be subjected to multifaceted critiques from a variety of sources, including orthodox psychoanalysts, feminists, experimental psychologists and historians.

The Eriksons returned to Cambridge, Boston in 1987. Part of the reason for their move was that Harvard University, amid some controversy, had set up a centre named after them and also provided them with a reasonable pension. Soon after, however, Erik's mind began to deteriorate noticeably – probably the onset of Alzeimer's disease. He and his wife Joan sold their Cambridge house and eventually Erik moved into a retirement home where he died in 1994.[1]

Erikson's work very much follows the pattern of his life and experiences. His first paper – on psychoanalysis and education – written in Austria, arose from his work as a teacher. His initial publications in the USA were concerned with the observations he had made of children's play and of education in Sioux and Yurok societies. The ideas contained in several of these early papers were drawn together in his first and best known book

Childhood and Society (1950),[2] which was published when Erikson was 48. The book focuses on the complex relationship between individual development and cultural and historical context and the mediating influence played in this process by methods of child rearing and education. It also introduces several other themes including his conceptions of the life cycle and identity which Erikson pursued in later writings. His interest in biography and historical context found full expression in two books or 'studies in psychoanalysis and history', *Young Man Luther* (1959)[3] and *Gandhi's Truth* (1969).[4] His ideas on identity and on adolescence are gathered together in *Identity: Youth and Crisis*[5] published in 1968. A number of his books have consisted of collections of previously published essays or lectures. In 1959 came *Identity and the Life Cycle*[6] and in 1964 *Insight and Responsibility.*[7] These were followed in the 1970s by *Life History and the Historical Moment* (1975)[8] and *Toys and Reasons* (1977).[9] Their titles hint at their contents. They include papers on clinical procedure and on Freud and psychoanalysis. Mostly though they develop and enlarge on the three primary themes which run through his work: *psychological growth and development throughout life, psychosocial identity* and the *study of individuals against the background of their time.* Each of these will be explored in turn in the chapters which follow.

The value and relevance of Erikson's contribution will be considered more fully in the final chapter where we will also take up in more depth the relation between his personality, life and work. At this stage though it is worth noting that it will be argued that, although his interest moved away from instinct theory towards the development of ego and identity, Erikson's achievement is in effect to deepen and extend the spirit of Freud's work rather than to offer a fundamental variation on it. In particular, his impressionistic approach effectively demonstrates the *hermeneutic* power of psychoanalysis – its capacity to provide insights into the complex subtleties of, in Heidegger's phrase, 'being-in-the-world'. He also shows how it can help to *integrate* our understanding of the complex factors which underlie individual being. These two functions, it can be argued, are psychoanalysis' most potent qualities.[10] Both will be demonstrated as this account of Erikson's work proceeds. Before going on to explore each of the three main themes noted at the end of the paragraph above, we will look in the next section more directly at his concern for integration by introducing his notion of *'triple book-keeping'.*

3 Triple Book-keeping

Erikson's first book *Childhood and Society* was first published in 1950 when he was 48. It went on to become the most important and influential of his publications and it was largely on this book that his reputation was founded. It represents the most explicit statement of Erikson's general position and approach and provides an excellent starting point for the reader who wants to understand the essential nature and variety of his ideas as well as appreciate his style and method.

As the title suggests, the book is focused on development in childhood and how children's emerging identities are interwoven with the fabric of the culture in which they live. It also takes up the notion of ego identity and how this develops through the course of life. To explore these themes Erikson brings to bear a rich set of topics and ideas, most of which he had already published earlier in the form of papers. Over the next two chapters we will explore in detail these interrelated topics; they include elaborations on Freudian theory, supplemented with observations based on Erikson's research work on children at Berkeley, the anthropological studies he had made of the Sioux and Yurok, and even the essays on Hitler and German society from his wartime work. In many respects, these summarize his thinking and work experience up to that time, and reflect the influence of people he had come into contact with – in Vienna, for example, and at Harvard. He also drew on his own experience of American culture as an immigrant. A key feature is the use of case studies primarily drawn from his clinical work with children. The detailed examination of these reflects one goal of Erikson's book – not just as a book for the general reader but as a training supplement for clinicians as well. The book however, is no pot-pourri of unrelated themes. A major feature is the attempt to interrelate the different facets which contribute to the construction of an individual's personality.

Triple book-keeping

This concern for interrelating different facets is made very clear early in the book. To understand an individual's actions or feelings at any moment in time requires, Erikson argues, taking into account three sets of factors: *somatic process or constitution* (that is, the physiological processes on which behaviour and experience depend), *social context* (the meanings and significances which society provides) and *ego process or identity* (the way a person resolves conflicts and makes sense of him or herself and the situation). Erikson emphasizes that these three processes are interdependent. Each is both relevant and relative to the other two. For effective exploration of the roots of behaviour, each must not only be viewed in turn but also in relation to the others. In other words, we need what he calls '*triple book-keeping*'.

> We are speaking of three processes, the somatic process, the ego process, and the societal process. In the history of science these three processes have belonged to three different scientific disciplines – biology, psychology, and the social sciences – each of which studied what it could isolate, count, and dissect: single organisms, individual minds, and social aggregates. The knowledge thus derived is knowledge of facts and figures, of location and causation; and it has resulted in argument over an item's allocation to one process or another. Our thinking is dominated by this trichotomy because only through the inventive methodologies of these disciplines do we have knowledge at all. Unfortunately, however, this knowledge is tied to the conditions under which it was secured: the organism undergoing dissection or examination; the mind surrendered to experiment or interrogation; social aggregates spread out on statistical tables. In all of these cases, then, a scientific discipline prejudiced the matter under observation by actively dissolving its total living situation in order to be able to make an isolated section of it amenable to a set of instruments or concepts.
>
> Our clinical problem, and our bias, are different. We study individual human crises by becoming therapeutically involved in them. In doing so, we find that the three processes mentioned are three aspects of one process – that is human life, both words being equally emphasized. Somatic tension, individual anxiety, and group panic, then, are only different ways in which human anxiety presents itself to different methods of investigation. Clinical training should include all three

methods. As we review each relevant item in a given case, we cannot escape the conviction that the meaning of an item which may be 'located' in one of the three processes is co-determined by its meaning in the other two. An item in one process gains relevance by giving significance to and receiving significance from items in the others.[1]

Erikson's clinical approach then is essentially *integrative*. He attempts to take into account the complexity and interaction of the three major processes – body, social situation and individual identity – which underlie human behaviour and experience.

Erikson illustrates this thesis by two case studies which 'highlight in an unusually dramatic way the principles governing the usual'.[2] They provide interesting demonstrations of his clinical method. One is taken from his work with psychological casualties from the Second World War.

A combat crisis in a marine

An ex-marine from the medical corps, in civilian life a teacher, was referred to Erikson because of his severe and persistent headaches and jumpiness. He had been evacuated from the Pacific war zone as a result of a 'breakdown' while under enemy fire. The patient could only talk about his experiences with difficulty and it was not easy to construct a coherent story from his recollections of what had happened. Apparently, he had been with a group of marines on an island and under heavy attack by the Japanese from the air. He was already feeling the debilitating effects of intestinal fever. Under the stress of the attack, a senior officer whom he much admired had uncharacteristically become abusive. To undermine his normal equilibrium further, the medic had 'found himself' with a sub-machine gun in his hands even though he had joined the medical corps precisely in order to avoid being in a position where he had to kill others. When night fell and the air bombardment intensified he gave way to total panic. This immobilized him and left him unable to offer any help to his fellow soldiers.

In working with his patient, Erikson first goes for specifics. What things, he wants to know, have been irritating him and bringing on his headaches in the last few days? The list of items given in response leads from the vibration of buses and the squeal of car tyres to thoughts of the traumatic experiences of battle and eventually to the memory of his mother.

In typical psychoanalytic style, Erikson begins to unpack the patient's early history. Once, when he was 14, his mother in a drunken rage had turned a gun on him. He had wrested it from her and left home never to see his mother again. He had been taken care of by the principal of his college – a man for whom he had much respect. Under his influence and perhaps in reaction to the experience with his mother, he had sworn never to drink or to touch a gun.

Given the pieces, Erikson's concern is to put them together. How do they cohere and make sense? Like the artist he once was, he feels for the total pattern or configuration. Erikson sees the marine's collapse as ensuing from a combination of failures in the different facets of his being. His *physical* debilitation laid the groundwork for his breakdown. This was exacerbated by disturbances in the *social context* – the rising anxiety and panic of the group aroused by the attack and the feeling of being let down by the forces they had expected to come to their aid. The marine strove to cope with these but was undermined further by events which upset his *sense of self* or '*ego identity*'. The superior he admired lost his composure and ordered him to take up a gun – something he had defensively avoided doing since he was a boy. These factors combined to produce his collapse. Evacuation as a result of his breakdown did not help his condition but rather intensified it by producing a lasting conflict between the desire to get away and feelings of cowardice and of letting the others down. Erikson suggests that in many such cases neurotic symptoms may satisfy an unconscious wish to suffer in order to assuage guilt.

The case of Sam

The other illustration is drawn from Erikson's therapeutic experience with children. Sam is a young Jewish boy who has suffered several epileptic-type, convulsive attacks although physical examination and family history reveal no reason to suppose that epilepsy was their cause. Erikson teases out the details of their onset. They had first occurred several years before when Sam was three. A few days after his grandmother died, Sam's mother had found him convulsed in bed, oddly enough supported by the pillows in just the kind of position his grandmother had favoured. The grandmother's death had come after several months of decline following a heart attack apparently brought on by Sam's naughty behaviour while she had been looking after him. More details about the occurrence of Sam's later attacks come to light – once after Sam had killed a butterfly, another on seeing a dead mole. Erikson traces the link between them and confrontations with death – in several cases death which might be attributed by Sam to his own actions. Erikson notes further evidence of Sam's aggressiveness and lack of restraint. He tends to fight with local boys and on one occasion knocked out his mother's tooth in retaliation after she had hit him when she had been upset. Erikson interprets the convulsive attacks he suffers as related to fear or guilt. They could represent for Sam a way of both venting his aggression and atoning for the feelings which he cannot control.

From the mass of details supplied by Sam, his mother and his own observations of them, Erikson feels for the overall pattern and the meanings which underlie it. He notes again the significance of the 'processes inherent in the organism'. By this he means that Sam is quite possibly constitutionally disposed to irritability and intolerance of restraint. To this consideration of *'somatic process'*, must be added concern with the *'organization of experience in the individual ego'* – in this case, the particular pattern of defences and adjustments which Sam has established. Assertiveness would be appropriate at his stage of development and his mother's own predisposition to give way to her angry feelings may well have encouraged this to take a more aggressive form. This pattern is then intensified by the *social milieu* in which Sam lives. Aggression is the accepted way in which the boys of the area relate to each other. An additional factor here might be the subterranean anxiety which any Jewish family living alone in a Gentile neighbourhood might be expected to feel, given the history of their people.

The essential flavour of Erikson's interpretative and therapeutic approach comes over clearly in these illustrations. The evidence he draws on is varied. He takes careful note of what his patient says and does and what others say about him. He is concerned to get precise details of the crisis and what leads up to it. He tries to discover the significant events and experiences in the patient's past life. In working with Sam he watches his play for hints of inner conflicts and concerns. He notes, for example, his fascination with using dominoes to build long boxes like coffins. At one stage, he even tests out his hypothesis that Sam has problems over self-restraint by playing a game with him and forcing him to lose. (Sam nicely provided confirmation by striking his therapist in the face!) While such participation by the analyst may be well removed from the neutral role of the orthodox Freudian, the tools and concepts which Erikson draws on are psychoanalytic enough. He acknowledges the significance of hidden motivations and defences. He looks for the underlying meanings which actions and words may symbolically represent and uses association to help guide him to his goal. He acknowledges too that a child's experience is qualitatively different. It is a world not yet as constrained by logic, conservation and causality as that of the average adult.³ To Sam, it is quite conceivable that it was his action that directly caused his grand-mother's death. Nor has the child yet developed efficient strategies of defence. He is very vulnerable.

Although in Sam's case the attacks diminished, Erikson lays no necessary claim to cure. He acknowledges that they could have cleared up anyway. What he does aspire to is to increase our understanding of what is happening in such a situation – knowledge which he hopes may provide support to help patients and their families to live with and work through the crises they confront. Erikson's approach then is *essentially* hermeneutic. He is not interested in establishing dogmatic laws. His goal is to make sense of the situation – to gain and convey insight into the complex of factors underlying a patient's actions and symptoms. It is the whole pattern of identity which concerns him, but many of its component parts are inaccessible, provisional, meaningless or even misleading taken out of context. So he has to put it together by what we might term a series of 'progressive approximations', and to cast his net widely – social milieu, physical health and ego development are all (to shift metaphors) very necessary grist to Erikson's mill.

This brings us again to the main point of these case examples. They are designed to demonstrate the need to take an *integrated* view – to look at all aspects which contribute to the construction of a person – biological, social and the experience of self, and to look at these each in relation to the others. This theme is reflected in the structure of *Childhood and Society.*⁴ First, Erikson considers the *somatic process* by elaborating on Freud's theory of psychosexual development. Next, with the help of his comparative studies of American Indian tribes, he illustrates the significance of the *societal process* and shows how, through the medium of child rearing, it can shape the individual. The section following that is then devoted to exploring the *growth of the ego* and evolution of individual identity. Let us look at Erikson's treatment of each of these in a little more detail.

Somatic process in psychosexual development

To illustrate the significance and role of biological processes in psychological life, Erikson uses the remainder of the first part of *Childhood and Society* to describe and discuss *psychosexual development*. Following Freud, he regards this as a process of progressive differentiation, during which the expression of a general drive is shaped as a result of the interaction of a biologically-programmed timetable of development with the way a child is handled by those who nurture him.

Erikson charts the sequence through which the child progresses. In Freudian theory, first comes the oral stage where the focus of interest is on the mouth and gratification comes from sucking and later, biting. As children become more capable of controlling their body functions, their attention turns to the anal area and they are likely to be required by parents to maintain some kind of control over where and when they excrete. The anal stage thus becomes the prototype for conflict between the child's desires and the demands of others. At about the age of four or five, interest begins to centre on the genitals, particularly on the question of anatomical differences between the sexes. In boys, the phallic stage is associated with the Oedipus conflict. The little boy's intensified feelings of affection for his mother conflict with his sense of rivalry with his father. Fear of both his own aggressive feelings and of arousing his father's anger are likely to lead to anxiety about injury. Given his child's imagination coupled with his focus of interest on the genitals, this usually takes the form of 'castration anxiety'. The Oedipus conflict is alleviated by repressing his incestuous feelings and by increased identification with his father. This in turn lays the foundation for the development of conscience or superego. Freud's account of the development of girls is more sketchy and controversial, and hinges on the notion of the disappointment and envy aroused by the little girl's discovery that she has no penis. A key effect of this, Freud believed, is the transferring of her main affection from her mother to her father, thus laying the basis for her future sexual role.

Like Freud, Erikson claims that the body mode associated with each phase (e.g., sucking at the oral passive stage) has its related psychological modality (e.g., passivity, desire to take in). So psychological characteristics emerge out of biologically-based actions, and, like them, evolve in a process of progressive differentiation. The attainment of psychosexual maturity is marked by the integration and subordination of infantile patterns to genital modes (e.g., orgasm) and genital modalities (e.g., mutual care). Neuroses and perversions arise as a result of fixation or regression to pregenital patterns. In this way, according to Freudian theory, many characteristics of adult personality are based on infantile development.

In many respects, Erikson's account represents no more than an effective restatement of Freud's ideas on psychosexual development. But he does add one or two ingredients to enrich the theory. For example, he clarifies the *epigenetic* nature of the sequence – how each stage grows out of the preceding ones but is qualitatively different in spite of its dependence on them. (As a developmental physiologist, Freud, as Erikson points out, would have been only too familiar with this notion.) Erikson draws a useful analogy with the physical development of the foetus. As each organ develops in the womb at a particular time and place, so also with psychosexual development. And like the emergence of physical organs, each phase is interdependent. If, for whatever reason, the expression of one is flawed, then the others are likely to be affected too. In his use of this analogy, Erikson encourages us to think of psychosexual development as a continuation of the maturation process started at conception. 'The maturing organism continues to unfold by developing not new organs, but a prescribed sequence of locomotor, sensory and social capacities...'[5]

Another contribution of Erikson is to devise an 'epigenetic chart'. With a series of schematic diagrams he plots the modes operative at each phase of development. Although he admits to its very generalized nature and the reader might be excused for wondering precisely what it adds, the chart does serve to draw our attention to the nature of this unfolding process. It makes it clear how at any stage the modes which characterize other phases are also present, if in subordinate and auxiliary form. As one example, the anal modes of elimination and retention may show themselves at the oral stage in the form of spitting out or refusing food. Like Freud, who had hinted at the possibility of some genetic basis for personality differences, Erikson makes the suggestion in passing that the degree to which such subordinate modes find expression may be a question of inherited temperament. This interplay of zones with modes characteristic of other phases is particularly likely to occur, of course, when there is regression. What the chart helps us to see then is that psychosexual development represents a *successive differentiation* of behavioural and psychological modes rather than a straightforward sequence where one phase is simply succeeded by another.

Although Erikson acknowledges Freud's achievement in formulating the theory, he points out that the concept of libido as pleasure-seeking energy should be regarded as metaphorical. 'Great innovators always speak in the analogies and parables of their day'.[6] In this case, Freud chose the language of thermodynamics – the study of the transformations which energy can undergo – to give form to his idea. A feature of Erikson's approach is his ability to stand back and see the bases from which a piece of research or a concept or assertion has been generated – to assess, in other words, its epistemological origins and status. This skill he is able to apply freely to his own work as well as to that of others. So he notes the process of selection that must inevitably underlie the charting of behaviours for each stage of his epigenetic chart and wryly comments in illustration on the series of photographs used in Arnold Gesell's classic *An Atlas of Infant Behaviour*.[7] These deliberately excluded several photographs of the naked boy model in which his penis was erect for 'such behaviour was not invited to the test: it has, as it were, crashed a good, clean party'.[8] While at Yale he had worked for a time with Gesell and had broken with him on just this issue and after Gesell had refused him access to the clinic's records because he considered Erikson focused too much on sexual aspects.

Another important ingredient stirred in by Erikson is his stress on the *mutuality* of the relationship between a child and his parents. This is not a one-way process of influence. Each is capable of affecting the other, as subsequent formal research has amply confirmed.[9] Erikson thinks of the phases of development not in a unilateral way but as a 'series of potentialities for changing patterns of mutual regulation' between parent and child. As the child grows older so the pattern of the relationship requires continuous adjustment. Problems arise if either parent or child fail to fulfil their needs in a reciprocally satisfying relationship but instead seeks to impose on or manipulate the other. In such a situation children may have recourse to fantasy or may use their body functions to express resentment or force a parent to comply. The aim of family psychotherapy then becomes 'to re-establish a mutuality or functioning between the child patient and his parents so that instead of a number of fruitless, painful and destructive attempts at controlling one another, a mutual regulation is established which restores self-control in both child and parent'.[10]

A great value of Erikson's account is its rich and subtle character. He presents no cold abstract scheme but rather shows us how psychoanalytic theory can work. In his hands it becomes not just a set of labels but living concepts which we can take and use to make sense of the children and adults we know. This may be due in no small part to the fact that Erikson did not, like Freud, have to reconstruct his account of early development from the recollections of adults. His work as a therapist and researcher was with children of all ages and his exposition of psychosexual theory rests directly on this experience.

The case of Little Peter

In *Childhood and Society*, his account of psychosexual theory is set, in typical Eriksonian style, within the framework of two case studies of his young patients. These are used to illustrate in particular how physical modes can be used by a child to express deep distress and concern. Little Peter, for example, was referred to Erikson because of his continuous constipation – when Erikson saw him he had not passed faeces for a week. This condition had been compounded by the achievement of getting a large object stuck irretrievably up his anus. Erikson employs his customary approach, gently talking and playing with the child, responsive to his actions and interests, all the time carefully observing, feeling for consistencies of meaning which connect his play and what he says. The underlying theme which Erikson detects is Peter's concern over the departure of a young and beloved nurse. From his mother's account it seems that Peter as a baby had characteristically expressed resistance through retentive behaviours – first by holding food in his mouth, later by sitting on the toilet without producing until she was forced to give up trying to get him to go. Now his reaction to distress at the loss of his nurse is to 'hold on'. Erikson sees Peter's symptoms as embodying a whole set of different though related meanings. As such, they represent a good example of the psychoanalytic notion of *overdetermination.* At one level, they could be seen as a physical expression of Peter's resolution to hold on tightly as a way of avoiding further loss; on another, as a symbolic identification with the supposed pregnancy of his nurse (she had told him she was leaving to have a baby). Yet again, they could be seen to represent a regression to a more infantile mode – expressing that he too is a baby and still needs her care. Erikson talks with Peter and explains about babies, gently exploring the boy's own fantasy of being pregnant and how this could not in reality be the case. His efforts appeared to have effect – at least Peter produced a superhuman bowel movement the following day. But the point at issue in Erikson's account is not therapy but understanding – showing the way a physical zone and its related modes may be used as an expression of psychological concerns. In all this Erikson refuses to ignore complexity. His account is not pat, the ends are not neatly tied – but then nor is this the case in life. If the vitality of the original personality is not to be squeezed out in reconstruction, that is perhaps the way it must be.

Another measure of the richness of Erikson's elaboration of Freud's libido theory is his occasional intriguing aside. In commenting on children's need at the teething stage to learn to suck without biting, he speculates as to whether this might not represent the ontological source of the ancient story of the Garden of Eden. Could the withdrawal of the breast in response to the child's sharp teeth be the prototype, he wonders, for the otherwise rather odd idea that God's wrath and human downfall was consequent upon biting into an apple?

Sexual differences in the organization of play space – a morphological basis?

Erikson is distinguished from many, if not most, other psychoanalysts by his experience as a researcher and academic. Another (though in some ways more questionable) contribution he makes to the issue of psychosexual development and the relation between behaviour, experience and bodily functioning, is to bring to bear the findings of a two-year study carried out during the longitudinal research project on Californian children which he was engaged on just before and during the war. While he introduces and briefly describes this in *Childhood and Society,* he elaborated on this later in a paper prepared for a symposium on the 'Woman in America' by the American Academy of Arts and Sciences called 'Womanhood and the inner space'.[11] The subjects of the study were 150 girls and 150 boys aged between ten and twelve. They had been coming to the clinic for assessment and observation for most of their lives. The goal of Erikson's study was to explore significances in children's play. One of his methods when working with children was to observe the way they used their toys, on the assumption that their constructions were likely to reflect their experiences and concerns. How far was this true? Erikson saw the children in turn and followed a procedure used previously with his students at Harvard. Each was presented with a set of toys – figures of people, animals, furniture, cars and building blocks. Their instructions were to create 'an exciting scene from an imaginary motion picture' and to tell a story about this. The wording was intended to circumvent any feeling that the subjects might have had that playing with toys was a task suitable only for younger children.

Erikson had biographical details of each of his subjects and so was able to compare these with the scenes and stories produced. Although he provides no formal analysis of the correlations between them, he does give examples of the kind of correspondences he claims occurred. A slightly-built black boy constructed his scene *under* the table in 'stark and chilling evidence of the meaning of his smiling meekness: he "knows his place"'.[12] A girl suffering a serious illness and supposedly ignorant of the fact created a ruin around a doll she describes as 'miraculously returned to life after having been sacrificed to the gods'.[13]

What particularly interested Erikson though was not so much the individual patterns but the many features he found in common among the productions of children of the same sex. Thus girls' constructions typically consisted of low enclosures of some kind, often representing house interiors or domestic scenes. Figures, usually female, featured in the scene but not very much appeared to happen except that not infrequently an animal intruded to upset things in a slightly threatening but at the same time humorous way. Boys, in contrast, characteristically used the blocks to erect high structures representing towers or buildings and the action of their stories often revolved around the dangers of collapse. A common activity was moving cars and animals around the streets usually under the control of the toy policeman, the figure they tended to use the most. Erikson points out that the differences are not just of configuration but of place and function. The concern of girls is with interiors, the key aspect of which is 'open' and 'closed'. For boys it is with action, almost all of it outside, and a preoccupation with height, with 'up' and 'down'.

Erikson confirmed his observations by giving photographs of the play constructions to colleagues who had no knowledge of the children who had created them. Erikson claims that more than two-thirds of the constructions were classified as fitting the criteria appropriate to the sex of their creators and that, for many of those that did not fit, there were factors in the children's personal histories which could have accounted for their atypical nature.

He accounts for such differences between the sexes by regarding them as rooted in their experiences of being male or female. In a passage which later became the target of vigorous feminist attack he points out their similarity to morphological and functional differences in the procreative process.

> ... Sexual differences in the organization of a play space seem to parallel the morphology of genital differentiation itself: in the male, an external organ, erectable and intrusive in character, serving the channelization of mobile sperm cells; in the female, internal organs, with vestibular access, leading to statically expectant ova.[14]

Of course, other explanations are possible. The patterns may merely reflect social influence – role identifications and activities learned by the children as being appropriate to their sex. Erikson does not deny this possibility. He merely asserts that it is insufficient to account for the data observed. The figures used and events created, he argues, are not especially representative of the children's worlds. Why should girls construct fewer and lower walls? Why should cowboys and pilots be selected so much less frequently than policemen when they would seem equally, if not more, acceptable role models for boys in wartime? Among other points, he also makes reference to the different uses of space between the sexes in other species; the tendency of baboons, for example, to enclose the females and the young in the centre of a protective circle of the younger, active male animals.

Such arguments may well not seem adequate to counter the suggestion that the differences observed could be a function of social influence. Erikson does seem to assert a very direct relation between biological functions and the use of space. When discussing his findings at least, he appears to pay insufficient attention, for example, to the very powerful effects of parents' responses to the sex of their offspring and how this may influence the child's preference for different forms of play. At any rate, in a later paper 'Once more the inner space',[15] he felt obliged to reinforce his position by answering the criticisms his writings on this topic had garnered from feminists. Erikson does not claim to have *proved* a connection between spatial modalities and bodily functioning, only that such a thesis is plausible and consistent with the evidence. Although different spatial modalities may 'come more naturally' to males and females, it is not his intention to suggest that either are doomed to be bounded by those more common to their sex. He is not resuscitating, he claims, Freud's dictum that 'anatomy is destiny'; his thesis rather is that 'history, personality and anatomy are our joint destiny'.[16] He goes on to reiterate the primary theme we are exploring in this chapter that 'each of the three aspects of human fate – anatomy, history and personality – must always be studied in relation to the other two, for each co-determines the others'.[17] Although experience may be 'anchored in the ground-plan of the body', a personality is 'an organic whole which cannot be broken up without a withering of the parts'.[18] Thus, although each aspect may have to be looked at in turn, 'only a total configurational approach – somatic, historical, individual – can help us to see the differences of functioning and experiencing in context, rather than in isolated and senseless comparison'.[19] So while somatic process may set up predispositions, these are then shaped and given meaning by the society in which individuals live. The exploration of how this happens becomes the next stage of Erikson's task.

Social context – Studies of the Sioux and Yurok

Perhaps partly as a result of his own change of cultures, Erikson began to take a considerable interest in social anthropology soon after his arrival in America. To elaborate the second theme in the triple book-keeping process and demonstrate how cultures knead and give meaning to the biologically given, he was able to draw on data he had gathered earlier on two field trips. In 1938, while at Yale, he had accompanied the anthropologist Scudder Mekeel on a visit to the Sioux in South Dakota. Later, during his stay in California, he had driven North with Alfred Kroeber to the Klamath River to stay with Yurok Indians who live on the Pacific coast. In both cases Erikson was able to rely on the help and mediation of two experienced guides and could draw on a body of historical data on the tribes in question. His particular contribution was to bring to bear his own brand of sensitive observation and illuminative insight and, with the help of psychoanalytic concepts, to put observations and other evidence together in a coherent and meaningful configuration. While the studies form Part 2 of *Childhood and Society,* both had been published previously as papers and as a monograph.[20]

Erikson sets about investigating a society much as he does an individual. He asks questions, listens and observes and tries to make sense of it all. His aim is to detect the key psychological dimensions which characterize the culture – its particular integrated pattern of values, beliefs, behaviours and relationships. His attitude is functional and ecological. He sees this pattern as related to the particular style of life which has been necessary for the tribe to survive. Any cultural configuration he regards as rooted in geographical, economic and historical necessity. He also considers the experiences of childhood as the important mediating influence by which the cultural pattern is maintained.

The Sioux – Hunters across the Prairie

The few thousand Sioux living on the reservation represented the forlorn survivors of a tragic history. Once a proud people, skilled at hunting and known for their daring and cruelty, their way of life had been gradually eroded by the coming of the white man. First he had decimated, often wantonly, the herds of buffalo. On this animal the existence of the Sioux depended. Its flesh yielded their food, its skin their clothing and shelter, its bones and sinews their utensils. Even the droppings were used for fuel. Then came the invasion of their lands and sacred hills by miners in search of gold. A series of skirmishes and sometimes bloody battles between the Sioux and the white intruders climaxed in the massacre of 1890 when, outnumbered four to one, most of the tribe including women and children were slaughtered by the US cavalry even though many had attempted to surrender. Those who remained alive had been forced onto reservations. There, their traditional style of life was totally undermined. They were not allowed to herd cattle for fear of upsetting the settlers' interests. They were forced to live by farming the arid land – a form of work quite alien to them. Their customs had been further weakened by the imposition of a foreign education system on their children. The introduction later of more humane policies brought them provisions but did nothing to alleviate the dissolution and apathy which reservation life induced.

Erikson gathered his information in a variety of ways. The Indians he talked with were not very forthcoming at first but eventually the older women in particular began to open up about traditional Sioux life and the ways they would rear their children. Erikson observed both daily activities and special social gatherings. Another source of information was an interracial seminar where teachers and social workers, mostly white, talked about the problems they encountered with the Indian children in their charge. Their concerns, Erikson noted, seemed to centre on the children's lack of respect for poverty and cleanliness, and what they regarded as their undue sexual activity, apathy and lack of initiative.

Erikson views these concerns against the background of the respective cultures – white and Sioux. Their traditional values are very different. For the Sioux, possessions have no virtue in themselves and are more likely to be a source of disdain rather than status. Generosity is a fundamental principle. Goods have value only in that they bestow the owner with the right to give them to others. As a nomadic hunting tribe, such a principle was appropriate to their situation. Extensive possessions could only be a burden on their travels. The group depended too for their survival on the beneficence of the most skilled of their members at catching game. Individual prowess was placed in the service of group need rather than individual aggrandizement. The Indian child's disinterest in competitive games reported by the teachers at the school is not surprising then, given the cultural climate in which they still grow up. What was seen as 'lack of initiative' may also be attributable to this.

White American notions of hygiene clearly had little relevance either for a nomadic tribe like the Sioux. In the past, a site would have been abandoned before it could become polluted. In the Indian method of hygiene, bodily waste and even corpses were 'given over to sand, wind and sun'.[21] The Sioux maintained a set of avoidances nevertheless – for example, those centred round menstruation. Mekeel reports the conflict faced by a typical Indian girl who might return from a government school, washed, cleanly dressed and with cosmetics on her face, only to be confronted by accusations from her mother of being a 'dirty girl' because of her failure to follow monthly taboos on handling foods.

To understand how traditional patterns can be perpetuated even today when the whole basis of the Sioux's existence has been forcibly altered, Erikson turned his attention to childhood experiences. They and their effects are interpreted in line with psychoanalytic theory but Erikson notes, after talking with the older Indian women, how closely such predictions accord with the reasons they give for bringing up children as they do. From birth the infant is 'spoiled' and fed whenever he or she demands. Breast feeding may go on for several years even when the child's diet consists largely of other foods. Such unlimited early satisfaction is interpreted as laying a basis for later generosity and self-confidence – the expectation that the world will meet all needs. Although the Sioux expressed disdain for the way that white people make their children cry, there is one exception to the generally permissive warmth that they showed towards their offspring. When infants develop teeth they may well be smacked and strapped down to a cradle board if they begin to bite at the breast. Crying at this stage is all right, the Sioux believe, for it will make a child strong. Erikson agrees, arguing that the fury provoked by the suppression of the desire to bite would provide a foundation for an aggressiveness which traditionally would have been redirected later towards enemies and prey; it also encouraged a fortitude in the face of pain which is very much part of the character of the Sioux.

At the anal stage, children learn what to do by copying the behaviours of older children. Such training by example rather than by prohibition is a general feature of Sioux rearing practices. Erikson claims that this fosters a strong sense of individual autonomy. Children learn to behave appropriately because they choose to do so, not because they are forced. The emphasis at the anal stage on free release rather than holding on also translates into the characteristic disinterest in possessions.

Soon after the fifth year, boys and girls follow different paths. The forms of play they engage in herald their respective later roles as Sioux men and women. Girls are taught sewing, cooking and tent construction. Decorum and caution are emphasized in relations with boys and men. Boys are schooled in hunting techniques. Self-confidence and loyalty to each other and the tribe are cultivated. They are encouraged to express aggressiveness towards legitimate 'prey'. Erikson sees this training as developing the characteristics whose foundation was laid during infancy. Influence is exerted largely through the forces of praise and ridicule. While this preserves a sense of autonomy (in comparison, say with the use of punishment), the important source of control remains the attitudes and acceptance of others rather than an inner conscience.

Even if we assume that Erikson's observations were accurate, his interpretations of them remain open to question. They rest, for example, on the propositions and assumptions of the psychoanalytic theory of psychosexual development. The considerable research effort which has been expended on attempting to validate these has led to rather mixed findings. The general conclusion is that, although they are not without foundation, they are still open to some doubt.[22] Erikson makes it quite clear though that he is not asserting a simple causal relationship between child-rearing practices and the dominant psychological characteristics of the tribe. He sees the situation rather as a 'mutual assimilation of somatic, mental and social patterns which amplify one another and make the cultural design for living economic and effective'.[23] Childhood experience facilitates the development of appropriate individual identities which, in the original context in which the tribe existed, provided a 'coherent design for living' which worked 'economically, psychologically and spiritually'.[24] Erikson's skill lies in the imaginative way he is able to construct the configuration of Sioux society as a model of this complex process. His interpretation points up the cohesive, interrelated nature of the fabric of a tribal culture – how the configuration is revealed, for example, in its toys, its rituals and beliefs. The phallic-like small buffalo bones, which Sioux boys love to play with for 'horses' and 'bulls', he interprets as a stimulus to their competitive and aggressive day-dreams. In the Sioux Sun Dance, a festival of feasting, games and sex, young braves traditionally inflicted torture on themselves by pulling against thongs tied to skewers stuck through the muscles of their chest and back. This Erikson interprets as:

> ... symbolic restitution necessitated by a critical experience which once upon a time caused an intense conflict between his rage against the frustrating mother – and that part of him which forever feels

dependent and in need of faith, as assured by the love of parents in this world and the parental powers in the supernatural.[25]

Though the form it takes will vary according to specific religious beliefs, such a sense of sinfulness is pervasive in many cultures. Its developmental origins lie, Erikson believes, in the 'paradox of orality and its loss during the rages of the biting stage'.[26] As we have seen, this is one time when the Sioux may frustrate their children.

In spite or perhaps because of its homogeneity, Sioux society makes available a place for deviants too. Interpretation of dreams might be used to 'officially' prescribe for the dreamer a specific role – in some cases outside the orthodox pattern for their sex. By attributing the source of such behaviours to the spirit who induced the dream, such deviations can be tolerated while still allowing for the resentment about deviance necessary for the majority to justify and sustain their more orthodox roles.

The Yurok – Fishermen along a Salmon River

The Yurok present a striking comparison. Their way of life changed little with the advent of the white immigrants from the East. Still they fish for salmon as they always have and dwell in clusters of villages along the largely inaccessible banks of the Klamath River. In marked contrast to the Sioux, the key mode in their culture is acquisition/retention. As befits fishermen, their primary concern is to catch and hold on to as much as they can get. They are skilled at fine economic transactions and were using shells as a medium of exchange long before they encountered notes and coins. Their concern for possessions spills over into their personal relationships. Erikson describes them as suspicious, petty and quarrelsome. There is little group feeling but, perhaps as a result of this, organized warfare is largely unknown.

Also unlike the Sioux, they have always lived in the one place. They travel little and show scant interest in what lies beyond the horizon. Given this settled existence and their dependence on fishing, avoiding pollution is clearly a relevant pursuit. Where for the Sioux the emphasis was on *strength,* for the Yurok it is on *cleanliness.* For them 'being clean' means avoiding contamination between the fluids from different sources and body channels. Their taboos prevent both urinating in the river and eating while fishing upon it, as well as demanding rituals of purification after sex.

As he was with the Sioux, Erikson is interested in relating the configuration of Yurok culture to their experience in childhood. He sees their child-rearing practices as focused on encouraging both oral and anal controls. Oral prohibitions start with the act of giving birth when the mother is not allowed to open her mouth. Breast feeding does not begin for ten days (nut soup is provided instead) and is soon over – certainly by the end of the first year and more usually before. This early weaning (in comparison with the Sioux) is followed by a series of injunctions concerning food. In a form of 'oral puritanism' not without precedent in our own culture, the Yurok child is required to eat without speaking and not to ask for more.

Although there seems to be little specific fuss about excretion during the anal phase, attention is paid to encouraging self-restraint and adherence to avoidance taboos. Another dominant theme of childhood is appreciation for economic concerns. While eating in silence, children are exhorted to think of salmon and how to become rich. Later, relationships tend to be strictly valued in economic terms and a prospective marriage is assessed for the monetary costs or benefits it will bring.

As before, Erikson is concerned to show how many different aspects of a culture will reflect its dominant concerns. The Yurok's fables tend to centre on the unfortunate consequences of self-indulgence. So the buzzard is said to have become bald because his head got soaked in hot soup as a result of drinking it too greedily. Even stories about the God of the Yurok carry a warning about giving way to temptation. He is reported as having been ensnared by the legs of the 'skate woman' after he had been tempted to seduce her. The Yurok's method of appeal to the spirits for a bountiful supply of salmon is to resort to tears. In this, Erikson claims to detect the residue of nostalgia for the lost breast which is typical in a child who has been weaned early. The climax of the Yurok year is the building of a communal dam to catch the salmon as they run upstream to spawn. In the Yurok equivalent of the Sioux Sun Dance, tears give way to gaiety and licentiousness. Every Yurok rejoices, 'proud that by an ingenious mixture of engineering and atonement he had again accomplished the feat of his world: to catch his salmon ...'[27]

Erikson's attempt to link childhood experiences and adult characteristics is less convincing in his account of the Yurok, at least viewed in strictly psychoanalytic terms. The Yurok personality seems anal enough with their stubbornness, stinginess, suspiciousness, miserly behaviour and compulsive rituals, but there is little evidence of other common concomitants of the anal syndrome such as anxiety about tidiness and time. Nor is there the concern about excretion in Yurok child training which one might expect from a strictly Freudian standpoint. But Erikson is viewing childhood experience with a wider lens. The particular feature of his approach, as we shall study more closely in the next chapter, is to consider the development of both children and adults in the framework of attitudes, beliefs and other aspects of the culture in which they live.

The analyses of both Sioux and Yurok are clearly highly speculative constructions. The reader is required to take Erikson's observations on trust. He has control over what aspects are selected for our inspection and how these are interpreted. More than one of his assertions give us cause to question. Why should the similarity of the Yurok's culture to our own make them more likely to be cynical towards us as he avers? The argument could just as easily be reversed. And when he writes of Sioux elders watching the antics of young men dancing jazz-style, as trying 'to hide pitying smiles behind their hands', it alerts us to the strong interpretative input that underlies his whole account. Nevertheless, although some specifics may be open to doubt, Erikson's overall achievement in these comparative studies is impressive. If this chapter has dealt with them at some length it is because no brief summary can do justice to the rich and complex analyses he presents. He does succeed in demonstrating the coherent configuration which a culture forms, how different elements – way of life, relationships, rituals, beliefs, even fables and children's toys – fit together and are expressive of underlying themes. His analysis would still be of interest as an illustration of this process even if it were hypothetical. It also shows how such a configuration *could* relate to childhood experiences and certainly helps us see more clearly the complex process whereby cultures elaborate on the pattern of individual growth.

Another function his analyses serve is to throw interesting light on the nature of cultural conflict and integration. The Indians and the white newcomers failed to understand each others' worlds for, as he puts it, each culture 'has its own particular logic which safeguards its coherence'.[28] But because the configuration of their culture, both psychologically and economically, fits quite closely to the 'Western' pattern, the Yurok remain a vigorous thriving tribe. The Sioux fare much more badly. While in the past there were white men whose place the Sioux could understand – the early hunters and even the cavalry who came to fight and parley with them – there is no equivalent in their tribal society for the bureaucrat and businessman. The traditional targets against which they could legitimately direct their aggressiveness are no longer there. It can only be turned against themselves, projected or displaced in 'antisocial' form. The traditional Sioux roles and values, such as disregard for property and refusal to engage in competition which are still fostered by the way their children are reared, find little place in a technocratic, capitalist world. Occasionally, they do fit – in occupations demanding daring, for example, such as a scaffolder or soldier in action. More often though they are out of tune in an alien context and result only in 'alignment with the lowest strata of our society'.[29]

The study of individuals against the background of their culture is a theme that continued to fascinate Erikson. From a somewhat different perspective, he took it up again in the studies of historical figures which we will be considering in Chapter 6. By stressing that individuals must be regarded in relation to their culture, Erikson is making clear that the Yurok are not to be considered as a tribe of anal neurotics in spite of the traits they show. For such a pattern enables them to function effectively in their social context, and there is no failure of ego functioning. It is the development of the ego which is the third factor in Erikson's trichotomy. To complete the picture of *triple book-keeping* we must now go on to consider this.

Ego development

The two preceding sections have illustrated the complexity of the *biological predispositions* and *social forces* which go to shaping our individual being. Our need for triple book-keeping makes it insufficient to rest our examination there. We need to look also at the process of *synthesis* – how we integrate them, particularly when their influences conflict, to establish a sense of unified identity – a cohesion and continuity in our experience of ourselves in relation to the world. This becomes the theme of Part 3 of *Childhood and Society*. Given Erikson's predilection for configurations, it is not surprising that the issue of synthesis and identity came to dominate his work. We shall unravel this, the third strand in the scheme, both in this section and in the next two chapters, as Erikson has approached it in his writings in several ways.

In traditional psychoanalytic theory the synthesizing function of personality is the ego. It was only towards the latter part of Freud's career that he directed specific attention to this topic. Erikson, though, had been trained by analysts like Anna Freud and Hartmann to whom it was of focal interest. Like Freud, they use the term ego to refer not, as in contemporary popular usage, to a sense of one's own self-importance, but to the 'inner synthesis which organizes experience and guides action'.[30] It denotes the processes of the psyche concerned with adjusting to 'reality' and with integrating the demands made upon it from both within and without. No mean task – for the power of the forces of id and superego, particularly in childhood, should not be underestimated, as psychoanalysis has been at pains to make clear. Erikson suggests that we can catch a glimpse of them if we take an honest look at our day-dreams, especially at moments of vague unease. We will probably become aware of a 'see-saw' between fantasies of omnipotent control, achievement or sexual licence and

> ... thoughts of 'oughtness': what we ought to be doing now in order to undo what we have done; and what we ought to do in the future instead of what we would wish we could do ... our irrational worry over 'spilled milk', our fear of having aroused actually quite disinterested, and antagonized quite well-meaning, people, our fantasied atonements and childish repetitions, may well surprise us.[31, 32]

In between, come moments of equilibrium when we neither wish anything to be other than it is, nor feel that we ought to. It is then, when the ego balances the see-saw cycle, that we are most ourselves.

Our waking fantasies, of course, tap only a few of the impulses and anxieties involved. More direct expression may come in our nightmares and our dreams. The world of children's imagination – their fantasies and fairy stories[33] – also provide more vivid hints of the powers of dread and desire that lurk within the psyches of us all. An individual's capacity to cope and come to terms with these rests on the strength of the ego. It is this which also provides, Erikson asserts, the basis of a sense of being, for 'in the social jungle of human existence, there is no feeling of being alive without a sense of ego identity'.[34] On the quality of our ego functioning rests also our sense of competence and self-esteem.

Jean – a case study of early ego failure

To illustrate just how indispensable the ego is to effective psychological functioning, Erikson discusses a case study of what he regards as the consequences of ego failure. Six year-old Jean was referred to him for a pattern of disturbed behaviours which would ordinarily be described as 'schizophrenic'. Erikson points out the difficulty which schizophrenic and autistic children have in using and responding to words like 'I' or 'you', which he attributes to a failure to develop a sense of integrated self. Jean showed little concern for relating with people, seeming to look through them and displaying more interest in machines like vacuum cleaners, and in pillows which she loved to hug and talk to. Her speech consisted almost entirely of obscure and repetitive phrases.

He at once suggested she return to her family from whom she had been living apart. This in itself seemed to produce a greater partiality for people – but of a literally 'partial' kind. For Jean developed a fascination for other people's parts, grabbing at her father's and brothers' genitals whenever she found the opportunity and clambering on her mother to poke at her breast.

Although Erikson makes very clear the difficulty of understanding the nature and origins of a condition of this kind, he suggests that one of the key elements involved is the failure of synthesis; that the pattern of Jean's behaviour illustrates

> … the essential ego-weakness which causes these children to be swayed at one time by a 'drivenness' focused on a part of another person; and at another by cruel self punitiveness and paralysing perfectionism. It is not that they fail to be able to learn, to remember, and to excel – usually in some artistic endeavour which reflects the sensory counterpart of their essentially oral fixation. It is that they cannot integrate it all: their ego is impotent.[35]

The ego then refers to the synthesizing, balancing processes of personality, mediating not only between drives and conscience but between private and public realms of existence. It operates at a largely unconscious level though it underlies the experience of self. It represents

> … an inner 'agency' safeguarding our coherent existence by screening and synthesizing, in any series of moments, all the impressions, emotions, memories, and impulses which try to enter our thought and demand our action, and which would tear us apart if unsorted and unmanaged by a slowly grown and reliably watchful screening system.[36]

Earlier writers on the ego focused largely on delineating mechanisms of defence which play a part in the screening and synthesizing process. In contrast, Erikson's interest is in understanding how such a complex capacity is attained – how does a healthy ego develop and by what means is it maintained?

The importance of play

For adults, reason and imagination – our capacity to remember the past and envision the future – have an vital role. With their help, we can work through conflicts in our minds and try out potential lines of action in fantasy and foresee inconsistencies or undesirable consequences. In ways like this, our thinking helps us co-ordinate and cope with the complexity of life. Where adults think or talk it through, Erikson believed that children play. Play for them is a vital activity on which ego development depends. He proposes that play essentially represents 'the infantile form of the human ability to deal with experience by creating model situations and to master reality by experiment and planning'.[37] In play 'aspects of the past are re-lived, the present re-presented and renewed, and the future anticipated'.[38] In support of his proposition he cites no less an authority than the mystic poet William Blake whose lines he draws on both for the preface and the title of *Toys and Reasons* (1977), his book on play:

> The Child's Toys and the Old Man's Reasons
> Are the Fruits of the Two Seasons.

Erikson is careful to distinguish the *play* of children from the *recreation* of adults. Adults at play are temporarily released from their involvement in a 'real world'. Necessity is replaced by the rules of a game. They cease to be bound by the pressures of time and often of normal modes of dress and comportment. But while 'the playing adult steps sideward into another reality', for children play is for real, by its means they are able to advance 'forward to new stages of mastery'.[39]

We have already seen how Erikson used play as a means of diagnosing psychological concerns when he was both working with individual children and also in his research on sex differences in the use of space. But here he is arguing that play serves far more than diagnostic purposes. It can be instrumental in both development and cure. He offers a case illustration of three year-old Mary who suffers nightmares and anxiety attacks. In Erikson's office she uses a doll to upend other toys. Suddenly she breaks off and calls for her mother. Erikson regards such play disruption as

signifying, like an adult's resistance, the surfacing too close to consciousness of traumatic feelings. After following up a complicated trail of clues,
he traces Mary's symptoms to a set of interrelated concerns – an early operation in which a sixth finger was removed, growing awareness of genital
differences between girls and boys, formal separation from her mother and
the possibility of a forthcoming tonsillectomy. But the crucial element in
her therapy becomes her ability to dramatize this in her play. So she con-
structs a stable built with blocks to look like a six-fingered hand and, as a
way of coming to terms with an earlier event in which her father had pre-
vented her normal habit of staying in the bathroom with him while he
shaved, she shuts Erikson in the room with her. In this kind of way, her
spontaneous play in itself, Erikson believes, helps Mary come to terms with
the problems she confronts.

How does play help strengthen a growing or struggling ego? For one, it
provides an arena in which children can try out new roles, exercise their imagination and acquire and practise skills. Sometimes too, Erikson agrees, it can
act as an outlet for buoyant energies and for cathartic release of repressed feelings. Most importantly though, it can help a child achieve a sense of active
mastery over events. Erikson illustrates this with Freud's description of the
play of his eight month-old grandson Ernst in his monograph *Beyond the
Pleasure Principle* (1920).[40] Ernst had devised a set of games – one involved
repeatedly throwing out of sight a wooden reel and then pulling it back again
by means of the string attached to it; another was making his reflection appear
and disappear in the mirror. Freud reasoned that these represented drama-
tizations of the disappearance and later return of his mother. Although her
absence had not appeared to distress him, this was because, Freud believed,
the child had been able to come to terms with it through his play. The throwing away expressed his growing autonomy and capacity to do without her.
In particular the child had transformed through his play a situation in which
he was a passive recipient into one where he had active control. (Freud, as
you may remember, also considered that 'repetition compulsions' – the continued dreaming or fantasizing about a past traumatic event – represented a
similar process of attempting to gain control over it.)

Children's play can also serve in more general and familiar ways to facil-
itate development of a healthy ego. Erikson employs a delightful account
from Mark Twain's *Tom Sawyer* in which Tom's friend Ben Rogers hoves
into view 'personating the *Big Missouri* ...' and being 'boat and captain and
engine-bells combined ...' In such ways, growing children explore,

synthesize and learn to become masters of themselves both in body and mind, while assimilating the images of their culture.

> One 'meaning' of Ben's play could be that it affords his ego a temporary victory over his gangling body and self by making a well-functioning whole out of brain (captain), the nerves and muscles of will (signal system and engine), and the whole bulk of the body (boat). It permits him to be an entity within which he is his own boss, because he obeys himself. At the same time, he chooses his metaphors from the tool world of the young machine age, and anticipates the identity of the machine god of his day: the captain of the *Big Missouri*.[41]

Play forms reflect the symbols of the society and age in which the child lives, be these steamboats or spaceships. They also change as the child grows older, marking the new statuses which come from initiations into school, into organized and competitive games, a gang or adolescence. Erikson also notes a general progression which involves a gradual extension of ego operations. The play of infants is *autocosmic* – that is, it is centred on sensual investigation of the world of their own body or the bodies and objects they come into contact with. Next, comes play in the *microsphere* of small toys where, in the imaginary worlds they create, children explore, learn and work through what interests or worries them. Eventually, play enters the *macrosphere* of activities with others – the world of shared games, fantasies and adventures. Older children who have access to all, learn what aspects of themselves can be played out in each realm. In keeping with psychoanalytic conceptions of development, Erikson considers that frustration or disappointment can lead to regression to an earlier phase. So if a child gets hurt in play with others, he may well retreat to 'overhaul his ego' in the microsphere.

While play continued to absorb Erikson's attention for 40 years, it is not the only process on which he considered the growing ego to depend. He stressed the significance of children's relationships. He also considered it vital that children feel that what they do is an accepted and valued part of the world in which they live. One problem confronting children in twentieth-century Western societies is that too rarely are they offered the 'opportunity to be a small partner in a big world'. The specialization of modern work and adult roles makes it more difficult for children to participate in the way that they can in more coherent societies like the

Sioux and Yurok. The world of children too easily tends to be split off and regarded as of little real account.

Erikson's analysis here points to the relevance for ego identity of social and historical context. Successful ego synthesis for both children and adults requires alignment with the social organization in which they live, for regular, mutual affirmation and validation by others, he claims, is a fundamental human need. Another basis for the development of a healthy ego is the availability of appropriate models for the child to identify with. Any social context offers only a limited range of models suitable as an aid to ego synthesis for a particular child at a given time.

Erikson uses the example of the five year-old son of a neighbour to illustrate the problems which can ensue where there is absence of an adequate ego ideal or where the models which are available are ambiguous. A series of violent actions by the small boy culminated in minor acts of arson. His father had deserted the family and had consequently been regarded with contempt by his mother and her female cousins who looked after the boy. Later in the war though, he became an air-force hero before eventually meeting his death in action. Erikson sees the effects of this on the boy as a confusing sequence of rejection followed by identification and rivalry, then compounded by guilt at his father's death. He attributes the boy's behaviour to the problems of ego synthesis posed by this confusion and his violent defence of whatever sense of integrated identity he has managed to forge. Again, play comes to the child's aid. His favourite activity became

> ... swooping down a hill on a bicycle, endangering, scaring, and yet deftly avoiding other children. They shrieked, laughed, and in a way admired him for it. In watching him, and hearing the strange noises he made, I could not help thinking that he again imagined himself to be an aeroplane on a bombing mission. But at the same time he gained in playful mastery over his locomotion; he exercised circumspection in his attack, and he became an admired virtuoso on a bicycle.[42]

Erikson's conception of the ego to denote the synthesizing and mediating processes of the personality is not fundamentally different from that of his predecessors and teachers. His contribution is, as with psychosexual theory, to bring the conception alive with detail and illustration. He is also concerned, as we have seen, to understand the processes which help to develop a healthy ego, especially the function of play and the relevance of social context. His achievement here, however, is not limited to this. He also documented the changing pattern of ego development through life and explored its role in the foundation of identity, particularly during adolescence. We go on to deal with each of these topics in turn in the next two chapters.

4 The Life Cycle

Erikson's most original contribution to the study of ego processes is his account of the 'Eight ages of man'. In this he shows that a strong ego has many aspects and that its development is a process which lasts throughout life. He first introduced the idea in *Childhood and Society*[1] but subsequently reworked and elaborated it in several publications, notably his books *Identity and the Life Cycle* (1959, 1980),[2] *Insight and Responsibility* (1964)[3] and *Identity: Youth and Crisis* (1968)[4] and a paper he contributed to Julian Huxley's volume *The Humanist Frame* (1961).[5] It also formed the substance of his lecture series at Harvard on the human life cycle. It is a theory which has provided an important stimulus for subsequent thinking and research on adult development.[6]

For many years Erikson had been reflecting on and reformulating Freud's stages of psychosexual development. In his concept of the life cycle, he goes well beyond Freud, adding stages to cover later childhood and adolescence, and also three stages to encompass development through adult life. He had been developing these ideas in the 1940s and the account he first published in *Childhood and Society* was based on a paper he gave at a 1950 White House conference on infancy and children. His wife Joan was an active collaborator in his thinking about the life cycle. As well as Erik's observation of his patients, they used reflection on their own and their children's lives as an important source of ideas.

In his account, Erikson charts the whole human life cycle (from 'womb to tomb' as his students labeled his course at Harvard) in terms of eight different phases of ego development. Each is characterized by a basic issue conceptualized as a pair of alternative orientations or 'attitudes' towards life, the self and other people. From the way the growing person is able to resolve each issue emerges a 'virtue'– a word used in its original sense by Erikson to denote a strength or quality of ego functioning. Thus, as we shall shortly see, the very first phase of life is characterized by the polarity of *basic trust versus mistrust* from the resolution of which emerges the ego strength of '*hope*'.

The sequence is seen, as before in his conceptualization of psychosexual development, as an *epigenetic* process; that is, the growth of the ego involves a progressive differentiation of interrelated characteristics where each, although existing in some form throughout, has a time of special ascendancy which is critical for its development. Erikson is suggesting an inner process of maturation that creates in each child and eventual adult a 'succession of potentialities for significant interaction with those persons who tend and respond to him and those institutions which are ready for him'.[7] Different qualities of ego strength then arise at different stages of a person's life. Erikson applies the term 'crisis' to these stages to indicate that each involves a fundamental shift in perspective which, although essential for growth, leaves the person vulnerable to impairment of the quality concerned. Each represents a 'turning point, a crucial period of increased vulnerability and heightened potential, and therefore, the ontogenetic source of generational strength and maladjustment'.[8] The word 'cycle' is meant to indicate that each individual life has its own overall pattern and, at the same time, forms a link in the continuous sequence of generations.

This is a novel contribution to psychoanalytic theories of development for it extends consideration to well beyond childhood and deals essentially with the processes of normal and healthy development rather than the aetiology of maladjustment. Erikson also succeeds in broadening the scope of his theory to take in not just frustrations and satisfactions but the whole pattern of a person's experience of life. He tries to indicate both the influence of family, friends and acquaintances and the part played by the wider culture.

In a later book *Toys and Reasons* (1977),[9] Erikson enlarged on the role of culture by discussing the place of '*ritualizations*' in the life cycle. By these he refers to *customary ways of doing things* – for example, prescribed ways of eating, looking after children, making atonements – by means of which a culture socializes its members into a particular version of human existence. By transforming needs into social actualities, ritualizations link the individual to the social order. But for each kind of ritualization Erikson describes, he also posits a negative form or 'ritualism' where the pattern has become so rigid or stereotyped that it is no longer conducive to ego growth. (Examples of these will be given in the discussion below.) A society is likely to offer ritualizations and institutions appropriate to the psychological requirements of each stage of human development, in this way making possible a mutual assimilation between individual growth and social process. With this notion Erikson thus seeks to develop his triple book-keeping theme that ego, biological maturation and social institutions interact and interrelate in the process of development.

Erikson's concepts are elusive and subtle. The quality of their meaning is sometimes adulterated by being summarized in more basic words. In the discussion of each stage that follows (and also of his concept of identity in the next chapter and his psychobiographies in the one following that) I have made liberal use of quotes. I have tried to capture the essence of Erikson's ideas in the way I have written about them. My aim is to give you, the reader, access to them without losing the subtlety and richness of meaning conveyed by his own writing.

1. Basic trust versus mistrust → Hope

The first stage more or less parallels the oral phase of Freudian theory. Its critical feature is the total dependence of the child on those who care for him. On their benevolence rests the satisfaction of his needs and the comfort of his existence. The quality of this care sets up an expectation, a *sense of basic trust or mistrust*. The foundations are laid either for an optimistic orientation to a world in which needs are satisfied, or a pessimism which comes to expect the worst. What is established then in this first year is a general attitude towards the self and the world. Erikson uses the phrase a 'sense of' to indicate its pervasive nature as an inner state which, like a sense of health or vitality, may be expressed through behaviour and, for the adult, may be at least partly accessible to introspective awareness. A sense of basic trust is founded on an association between feelings of comfort and consistencies in the external world.

> ... consistency, continuity, and sameness of experience provide a rudimentary sense of ego identity which depends, I think, on the recognition that there is an inner population of remembered and anticipated sensations and images which are firmly correlated with the outer population of familiar and predictable things and people.[10]

It also implies that 'one may trust oneself and the capacities of one's own organism to cope with the urges'. Erikson makes clear that the critical need here is the *balance* between trust and mistrust, to know when trust is appropriate and when danger or discomfort realistically threaten.

The essential virtue or ego quality which emerges from this phase is *hope*. Erikson defines this as *'the enduring belief in the attainability of primal wishes, in spite of the dark urges and rages which mark the beginning of existence'*.[11]

The opposing outcome is a depressive state involving excessive caution and withdrawal in relations with the world – an inability to trust others or oneself. If there is, for example, at weaning, too sudden a loss of the comfort of the breast and reassuring physical contact with mother, this may result in a depressive mood which may persist through life. In extreme form this may become a psychotic condition where all offers of human contact are rejected or ignored.

The social *ritualizations* of this stage centre on habits and practices of care and ways in which parent and child give attention to each other. Erikson sees such ritualizations as promoting in infants a sense of the *'numinous'* – amalgamated feelings of attraction and awe – which will lay a foundation for later participation in organized religion.

> Trust born of care is, in fact, the touchstone of the *actuality* of a given religion. All religions have in common the periodical childlike surrender to a Provider or providers who dispense earthly fortune as well as spiritual health.[12]

As remarked earlier, ritualization, in common with many of Erikson's concepts, has its negative form – in this case *pseudo-ritualization* or *ritualism*. Here, this takes the form of *idolism* – excessive adulation, for example, of religious figures. Erikson sees the expression of this as ranging from 'mere compulsive compliance with daily rules to the obsessive-repetitive expression of fanatic and delusional visions'.[13]

Interestingly, Erikson suggested that another social pattern which also reflects reliance or trust in faith is a delight in gambling and in taking risks. He was thus trying to link two seemingly very different kinds of social behaviour (that is, religion and gambling) by relating them to a common ontogenetic base. While this bold attempt is both thought-provoking and provocative, it would take more than the brief assertion which is all his argument constitutes, to establish a convincing case.

2.   Autonomy versus shame and doubts → Will

With the anal phase comes the beginning of a capacity for independent action. A focal concern of the parents is likely to be to encourage the child to exert self-control over excretion. But the issue of control by self or others and the anal modality of retention and elimination becomes generalized to many other aspects of the child's world.

> This whole stage, then, becomes a *battle for autonomy*. For as he gets ready to stand on his feet more firmly, the infant also learns to delineate his world as 'I' and 'you', and 'me' and 'mine'. Every mother knows how astonishingly pliable a child may be at this stage, if and when he has made the decision that he wants to do what he is supposed to do. It is impossible, however, to find a reliable formula for making him want to do just that. Every mother knows how lovingly a child at this stage will snuggle close to her and how ruthlessly he will suddenly try to push her away. At the same time the child is apt both to hoard things and to discard them, to cling to treasured objects and to throw them out of the windows of houses and vehicles.[14]

The reactions of parents to the child's first attempts at self-assertion sow the seeds for a later sense of *autonomy* as opposed to feelings of *shame and doubt*. What is crucial is balance and the ability to ensure co-operation without dominating the child's desire for freely chosen action.

> A sense of self-control without loss of self-esteem is the ontogenetic source of a sense of *free will*. From an unavoidable sense of loss of self-control and of parental overcontrol comes a lasting propensity for *doubt* and *shame*. [15]

The danger here is the destructive potential of shame and our defences against it.

> To learn to avoid being laughed at … means to learn to look at ourselves and our acts from outside and to adjust our will to the views of those who judge us. But this also demands the development of that inner self-watch which Freud called the super-ego, that is, literally a part of ourselves standing watch over the rest of ourselves and confronting us with detestable self-images. We thus learn to look down upon ourselves as unworthy and guilty, and are apt to do so with such cruelty that we sometimes feel relieved only when punished. Nor could we face ourselves did we not also learn to look down on others as we look down on creeping creatures. We can then

protest we are not the lowest, and can claim that we belong to the relatively elect.[16]

Shame can engender a corrosive self-doubt which can undermine the possibility of action and in extreme adult form lead to feelings of persecution because of the 'shamefulness' of one's ways. But balanced navigation of this phase results in the ego quality which Erikson terms – '*the unbroken determination to exercise free choice as well as self-restraint, in spite of the unavoidable experience of shame and doubt in infancy*'.[17]

The *social correlate* of this second phase is the *Law* (or the principle of the *Judicious*) which, if just, ensures a fair apportionment of obligations and rights. The ritualizations of this stage constitute the boundaries which children learn between the things they can and those they must not do. The negative face of ritualization is found in the self-righteous and legalistic niceties of those who prefer the letter to the spirit of the law.

3.   Initiative versus guilt → Purpose

If the first stage lays down a basic ability to trust in the world and others, and the second the capacity of children to have confidence in themselves as they are, then the third is concerned with how far children can learn to have *faith in their actions* and in what they can become. At this phallic stage children's powers are developing. They are getting adept in the use of language to obtain what they want and are capable of thought and planning as well as fantasy. They tend to be vigorous, active and into everything; as Erikson puts it, they are 'on the make'. But this is the time of the Oedipus complex – the heightening of superego development and control, and the child's growing sense of his own power is likely to be counterbalanced by fear of potential harm, symbolized by castration anxiety. So capacity for initiative may be undermined by fear of consequences or by guilt engendered by the moralistic controls exerted by the superego. Again, what is important here is a sense of mutual regulation, that children be allowed to assert themselves without being crushed by a sense of guilt at what they do or wish. Otherwise the consequence may be overobedience and conformity, the inability to act out what is desired. In adults, this may result in, as with hysterics, denial or repression of unconscious needs or at least an inhibited and self-restricted personality. But the outcome of the Oedipus stage is not only 'a moral sense constricting the horizon of the permissible; it also sets the direction towards the possible and the tangible which attaches infantile dreams to the varied goals of technology and culture'.[18] Balanced development here ensures that ego functioning develops a capacity for *purposefulness* – '*the courage to envisage and pursue valued goals uninhibited by the defeat of infantile fantasies, by guilt and by the … fear of punishment*'.[19]

The ritualization of this stage is managed through the *toys* which the child is given and which can be used to create miniature worlds where roles can be explored in play and actions initiated. (The adult arena for such dramatic realization is the *stage* – 'mature man's inspired toy' as Erikson would put it.) A further connection between this third phase and the social order lies in the *stories* which children are told, which offer them cultural templates for initiatives they themselves may someday sustain. Children are becoming aware too of the *roles which adults play*, particularly those, like train drivers, nurses or policemen, which are clearly signified by dress or function. If dramatic elaboration is the ritualization emerging from this stage then it also lays the foundation for its negative counterpart – the ritualism of *impersonation*. The key difference is authenticity. In impersonation, although the role is played as if for real, the part is assumed – as sometimes, for example, when a politician takes on the mantle of 'Statesman' or 'Great Leader', the player is not at heart the person he purports to be.

Although the first three phases are linked to those of Freudian theory, it can be seen that they are conceived along very different lines. The emphasis is not so much on sexual modes and their consequences as on the ego qualities which emerge from each stage. There is an attempt also to link the sequence of individual development to the broader context of society.

4. Industry versus inferiority → Competence

In almost all societies, some form of systematic instruction is provided for children beyond the age of five. For the first time, they move firmly outside the orbit of their family and into the wider world. In our culture, they go to school. Although Freud saw this as the latency period when the stormy emotions of the younger child abate for a time until the onset of adolescence, in social terms, as Erikson points out, this is a very decisive phase.

Recognition now begins to rest on the exercise of skills, and children may become aware of being judged on their performance in comparison with their peers. Where children feel inadequate to their task, a *sense of inferiority* may be the result and they may be deterred from testing out what they can do. But if a child is encouraged and given confidence, the ego quality which can emerge is a sense of *lasting competence* – the *'free exercise of dexterity and intelligence in the completion of tasks, unimpaired by infantile inferiority'*.[20]

The social order interlinks with this stage through educational activities which are likely to reflect its particular technological ethos. Ritualization takes the form of the methods which children learn as the correct way to perform their tasks. Thus 'play is transformed into work, games into competition and co-operation, and the freedom of imagination into the duty to perform with full attention to the techniques which make imagination communicable, accountable, and applicable to defined tasks'.[21] As usual, Erikson considers that such ritualizations come with their negative potential – in this case a *formalism* which emphasizes perfection of technique itself rather than the ends which the skill was originally designed to achieve. A related danger is that a person comes to place too great an importance on work and achievement, resulting in 'constriction of his horizons' so that 'he may become the conformist and thoughtless slave of his technology and of those who are in a position to exploit it'.[22]

5. Identity versus role confusion → Fidelity

The phase which in many respects had most fascination for Erikson is adolescence. This is the time of physical and social changes where developing a sense of *identity* becomes the focal issue. Young people are confronted with the need to make decisions as to what they are and will be. What jobs should they take? What attitudes should they hold? What kinds of relationship should they pursue? Who are they? How should they dress, behave, react? The boundaries which hitherto have kept them firmly in place now one by one become dissolved. They are confronted by the need to re-establish them for themselves and to do this in the face of an often potentially hostile world. Creating their own identity may require reacting negatively. It may mean actively denying those attributes and roles thrust upon them by other people like parents and teachers.

As Erikson points out, so much of the phenomena of adolescence is concerned with this establishing of identity, a search for people and ideas to have faith in, idolizing heroes, going together in groups, adhering to special styles and conventions of behaviour and dress – think of punks or goths and the loyal fans of pop groups, and rejecting deviants from their norm. There is an absorption too with how they appear to people significant to them. First relationships, as he also comments, are not just a matter of re-emergent sexuality. They are concerned with finding oneself through being reflected in the eyes of an intimate partner – which is why talking is so central in adolescent relationships. The problem of adolescence is one of *role diffusion* – a reluctance to commit which may haunt a person into his mature years. What a young person essentially needs, Erikson believes, is enough space and time to freely experiment and explore – he calls this a *psychosocial moratorium*. Given such conditions, what may then emerge is a firm sense of identity, an emotional and deep awareness of who he or she is.

Dependent on this stage is the ego quality of *fidelity – the ability to sustain loyalties freely pledged in spite of the inevitable contradictions and confusions of value systems.*[23] The corresponding part of the social order is *ideology* which offers sets of beliefs and values as guides to the development of identity. Ritualizations here comes in two broad forms:

Spontaneous 'rites' by which adolescents ritualize their relations to each other and demarcate their generation as (slightly or militantly) different both from the adult haves and the infantile have-nots...

and *'formal rites and rituals'*, by means of which

... adolescing human beings are enjoined to become responsible members of their society and often of an elite within it. Only then can they enter the process of becoming an adult in the sense that they can visualize a future in which they will be the everyday ritualizers in their children's lives and, perhaps, occupy ritual positions in the lives of the next generation.[24]

The negative ritualism is *totalism* 'a fanatic and exclusive preoccupation with what seems unquestionably ideal within a tight system of ideas',[25] a pattern to which the puritanical intensity with which a few young people maintain their membership of cults and ideologies bears testimony.

6.   Intimacy versus isolation → Love

Erikson segments adult life into three broad phases which are discussed in turn in this section and the two that follow.

First, following close on the heels of identity concerns comes – usually around the early twenties – the need to develop the *capacity for intimacy*. The essence of this is the capacity to commit oneself 'to concrete affiliations and partnerships and to develop the ethical strength to abide by such commitments, even though they may call for significant sacrifices and compromises'.[26] Intimacy may be sought in friendship, inspiration and love which can be shared with others, even, Erikson suggests, in combat (presumably he is referring here to comradeship in battle). As he points out, intimacy tests the firmness of the identity established, for deep involvement with another demands the strength to put one's own individual identity at risk.

> Body and ego must now be masters of the organ modes and of the nuclear conflicts, in order to be able to face the fear of ego loss in situations which call for self-abandon: in the solidarity of close affiliations, in orgasms and sexual unions, in close friendships and in physical combat, in experiences of inspiration by teachers and of intuition from the recesses of the self.[27]

While intimacy may take many forms, for Erikson sexual relations provide the supreme example. In Freudian theory the genital stage is the time when sexual patterns established in the early years of life re-emerge transformed into the modes of adult sexuality. But for Erikson it is much more than this. A central feature is the mutual search for a *shared identity*, 'finding oneself as one loses oneself in another'. He argues that it is only at this stage that what he calls 'true genitality' can develop, for until this time, sexual relations are more likely to have been in the service of the search for individual identity or a kind of proving ground for sexual prowess than a true intimacy. He also qualifies orthodox psychoanalytic views of genitality by insisting on the need to relate it to social organization. In complex societies there are likely to be many potential obstacles to the opportunity for attaining 'the kind of mutuality of orgasm which psychoanalysis has in mind'. Because of this, the notion of sexual health should be reformulated to include not only the capacity for orgasm but also for tolerating a degree of frustration 'wherever emotional preference or considerations of duty and loyalty call for it'.[28]

From the interplay of polarities at this stage comes the capacity for *love* which he defines as a *'mutuality of devotion forever subduing the antagonisms inherent in divided function'*.[29] The counterpoise of intimacy is *isolation* and self-absorption. Fear of encroachment on the essence of one's identity may lead to *distantiation* – where all efforts by others to initiate intimacy (particularly by those perceived as different in some essential way) will be rebuffed.

Almost all societies provide a major ritual to celebrate intimacy, in the form of *marriage*. Intimacies can also be seen to be fostered and protected by what he calls *affiliative ritualizations* – particular forms of communication and greeting and complicit allusions, the 'demonstrative display of shared tastes and predilections, of enthusiastic opinions and scathing judgments that so often pervade the conversations and actions of young adults bound in love or work, in friendship, or in ideology'.[30] Acting like the affiliative rituals of bonding birds, these serve to cement together a couple or group. The negative face of affiliative bonds is reflected in the 'shared narcissism' of the *élitism* of exclusive groups.

7.   Generativity versus stagnation → Care

The theme of Erikson's seventh age is *generativity*. As children are dependent on us so we are on them, for mature adults 'need to be needed'. The essence of generativity is 'the concern in establishing and guiding the next generation'.[31] This may not necessarily imply caring for one's own offspring although this is the prototypal form. Adults may give of themselves by teaching others their skills and knowledge. 'Every mature adult knows the satisfaction of explaining what is dear to him and of being understood by a groping mind',[32] and in such ways passing on to these other 'offspring' the fruits of their own work and creativity.

An adult who does not develop generativity, Erikson asserts, retreats instead to a stagnating and eventually boring preoccupation with self in which 'he becomes his own infant and pet'.[33] For couples this is likely to take the form of regression to an obsessive need for 'pseudo-intimacy' in which the partners indulge themselves and each other as if they were their child. While becoming a parent may make it more likely that the balance shifts in favour of generativity, in itself it by no means guarantees this.

Generativity implies a capacity to give without expectation of return. Erikson labels the ego quality which emerges from this stage as *care* – '*the widening concern for what has been generated by love, necessity, or accident; it overcomes the ambivalence adhering to irreversible obligation*'.[34]

Generativity is usually sanctioned by the social practice of marriage. It is often reflected too in religious symbols, as for example, the image of God as father and teacher. Interestingly, caring for and teaching others is often a cardinal feature of religious organizations even (perhaps especially) where celibacy is the rule. Erikson goes on to suggest sweepingly that all human institutions are caught up in some way in this process, for all provide a means of passing on what they represent to generations to come. Specific ritualizations are contained in those parental and didactic practices which clearly imply that mother, father, the school or the Lord is the real source of knowledge and arbiter of what is right. This becomes a negative ritualism when it takes on the character of what he calls an oppressive *authoritism* – 'a self-convinced yet spurious usurpation of authority'[35] – spurious because it is based not on the authority of authentic knowledge or experience but on mere assertion of knowing best.

8. Ego integrity versus despair → Wisdom

From the interplay of ego integrity versus despair comes the fruit of our final years – *wisdom, 'the detached and yet active concern with life itself in the face of death itself ...*'[36] While Erikson hesitates to define *ego integrity*, he indicates the kind of attributes it embraces – the quiet certainty of the ego's strength, accepting the nature and inevitability of the pattern of one's life and not seeking desperately for last-minute restorations. While appreciating the richness of variability in the ways in which life can be lived, and while realizing that 'an individual life is the accidental coincidence of but one life cycle with but one segment of history',[37] such a person is ready to stay with and assert the particular pattern which has come to characterize his or her own life. Lack of ego integrity is marked by *despair* – by agonized concern in the shadow of impending death over unrealized goals and unfulfilled potentials, sometimes expressed in disgust with life and other people. Only

> ... integrity can balance the despair of the knowledge that a limited life is coming to a conscious conclusion, only such wholeness can

transcend the petty disgust of feeling finished and passed by, and the despair of facing the period of relative helplessness which marks the end as it marked the beginning.[38]

Though the growth of secularism has tended to undermine our concern for finding meaning in human existence, the need for integrity is reflected in the social order by philosophy and the search for general understanding.

In traditional cultures, the aged were often prized for their knowledge and wisdom and ascribed an exalted place. There were complex ritualizations for soliciting their judgement and advice. (The degraded form or ritualism of this is the pretence of being wise; *sapientism* is Erikson's term.) Today, there is a less clear conception of the overall pattern of human life. Too often, Erikson feels, it is conceived of as a one-way street to 'success – and sudden oblivion', leaving no valued role for our elders to assume.

This last phase may be seen to complete the cycle. As Erikson elegantly phrases it,

> Webster's Dictionary is kind enough to help us complete this outline in a circular fashion. Trust (the first of our ego values) is here defined as 'the assured reliance on another's integrity', the last of our values. I suspect that Webster had business in mind rather than babies, credit rather than faith. But the formulation stands. And it seems possible to further paraphrase the relation of adult integrity and infantile trust by saying that healthy children will not fear life if their elders have integrity enough not to fear death.[39]

The nature of the scheme

What Erikson has provided us with is a sequence of critical periods in the human life cycle. By critical, you may remember, he is not implying any catastrophe but that they represent, as in the essential meaning of the term, crucial developments in which 'a decisive turn *one way or another* is unavoidable'.[40] The scheme is *dialectical* in character for the stages are conceived as a set of polarities or oppositional tendencies. Although these are generated by the process of maturation which fosters a growing readiness to engage with the world in a more differentiated way, Erikson postulates that society is organized in such a fashion as to respond to such potentialities

	1	2	3	4	5	6	7	8
8 OLD AGE								Integrity vs. Despair, Disgust: WISDOM
7 MATURITY							Generativity vs. Stagnation: CARE	
6 YOUNG ADULTHOOD						Intimacy vs. Isolation: LOVE		
5 ADOLESCENCE					Identity vs. Role Confusion: FIDELITY			
4 SCHOOL AGE				Industry vs. Inferiority: COMPETENCE				
3 PLAY AGE			Initiative vs. Guilt: PURPOSE					
2 EARLY CHILDHOOD		Autonomy vs. Shame, Doubt: WILL						
1 INFANCY	Trust vs. Mistrust: HOPE							

Figure 4.1 Erikson's *Life Stages* (From Erikson 1976). They are charted in this fashion to indicate the 'epigenetic nature' of Erikson's scheme. Each polarity and ego quality comes to crisis at the stage indicated. Each though exists in some form at the stages both before and after its crisis time. (See discussion in the text, p.57.)

when they occur and so to maintain the pace and order of their emergence. From the interplay at each phase emerges a set of qualities which demonstrates the strength of the ego in integrating aspects of inner life and the person's relationship with the social world. So individual and society are intertwined – these qualities serving to replenish the vitality of social institutions while at the same time being shaped by them.

Erikson is very concerned to refute any notion that what he is suggesting is a form of achievement scale. It is not simply that the positive pole of the pair is the attainment to be desired. All that Erikson will commit himself to is the desirability of establishing a 'dynamic balance' or 'favourable ratio' of the positive to the negative pole. Essentially, as a dialectic conception, they are to be seen as dynamic counterparts, each tendency playing a part in fostering the development of ego strength. So, for example, too firm a consolidation of identity at adolescence may close off the possibility of later flexibility and openness to change which may have to be paid for at maturity by painful readjustments.

The notion of epigenesis also makes clear that although each polarity and its emergent ego quality has its particular time of ascendance, it is not restricted to that stage and that alone. So, for example, once the capacity for hope has emerged it is likely to persist through life, though modifying its precise character according to the needs and conflicts which are salient at any particular time. Nor is an individual to be thought of as 'located' at any one stage. Rather, everybody oscillates between at least two stages and they are likely to move into a new phase only when a crisis of a yet higher one begins to enter into play.

As it stands, the scheme Erikson presents is a very generalized one and it generated considerable controversy over how universal the stages could be considered to be. Erikson made no attempt to trace differences in ego development between the sexes because he believed that, beyond childhood at least, there are few consistent differences in this respect. Some 25 years after its original formulation, Carol Gilligan (who had been one of Erikson's teaching assistants at Harvard) begged to differ. She made a strong case that female development follows a significantly different pattern than that of males. In particular she stressed the importance of personal relationships in female development and that the capacity for intimacy is more likely to precede the establishment of identity than follow it.[41] Erikson did accept though the possibility that his theory could be class or culture bound and, indeed, actively pursued that question not only through his anthropological studies but by setting up seminars (for example, in India)[42] to discuss and compare the pattern of the life cycle in societies different from his own.

There are certainly many details which remain to be elaborated. Erikson's discussions of the ritualizations of the three adult phases, for example, are somewhat sparse and flimsy. There is also a lack of rigour, which is perhaps inevitable, in the formulation of the phases. The behaviours and components are not easy to specify precisely and they are often unclear. Sometimes too they seem to overlap, though this may reflect the way things are rather than any inadequacy in the account. Erikson himself raised the question of the basis on which his scheme rests. Is it founded on clinical observation or does it represent 'a humanistic ideal with unavowed moralistic or esthetic demands impossible to live up to in daily life'?[43] He claimed that, while speculation is involved, it is by no means an entirely arbitrary scheme. It is anchored in his observations of the nature of individual psychological development and the sequencing of generations. In support, we might acknowledge that his therapy and research (as well as his private life) provided him with excellent access to intimate clinical details from people at all stages of life.

The scheme is best regarded, to adapt his own phrase, as *a tool to think with*, rather than 'a prescription to abide by'.[44] It serves to differentiate the varied facets of the ego in its role as 'a selective, integrating, coherent and persistent agency central to personality formation',[45] as well as drawing our attention to the mutual regulation between social organization and personal development. It has, I think, much potential personal relevance too. We become more aware of the 'miracles of everyday life' which ego qualities represent, and of the potentials and problems of the different phases of our life experience.

The power of the scheme as a tool to think with was beautifully revealed in Erikson's analysis (1976)[46] of Ingmar Bergman's film *Wild Strawberries*. The film narrates the long journey of the ageing Dr Borg from his home to the University of Lund where he is to receive an honorary degree. On the way, he encounters members of his family and acquaintances of different generations and muses on his dreams and on recollections of the past. Erikson takes the scenes from the film and shows how they can be seen to reflect the critical phases in the old man's life – 'his own terminal conflicts open up all his earlier ones, as personified by the younger persons who confront him (in fact or in fantasy) on his journey'.[47] So, for example, his son's resistance to his wife's desire for a child opens up his own unresolved conflict over generativity versus stagnation; and his reveries about his past, as well as the quarrel of a middle-aged couple picked up on the road, reawaken awareness of his own problems over intimacy. Interestingly, Erikson himself was later also to receive an honorary degree from the University of Lund.

In his subsequent writings, Erikson goes on to deepen his contribution to our understanding of the life cycle in two particular ways. One is represented by his *biographical studies* of the lives of specific individuals. The other, which we will consider first, is to elaborate in greater detail on the issue which first comes to ascendancy as we move into adulthood – *identity*.

5 Psychosocial Identity

Running throughout Erikson's work is the theme of identity. It is first intro-duced in *Childhood and Society*[1] and then becomes the subject of several individual papers and lectures. These are best represented in the collections *Identity and the Life Cycle* (1959)[2] and in particular *Identity: Youth and Crisis* (1968).[3]

There are several reasons why the concept assumed so much importance for Erikson. One is its significance in contemporary life. The nature of a society will be reflected in the psychological problems characteristically experienced by members of that society. In Freud's time, Erikson argues, inhibition and repression were predominant concerns. But the complexity, mechanization and rootlessness of contemporary industrial society has led to a shift in emphasis.

> The patient of today suffers most under the problem of what he should believe in and who he should – or, indeed, might – be or become; while the patient of early psychoanalysis suffered most under inhibitions which prevented him from being what and who he thought he knew he was.[4]

Identity confusion is, Erikson claims, the more important issue today. 'The study of identity ... becomes as strategic in our time as the study of sexuality was in Freud's time'.[5] There are clinical and theoretical reasons too, for it is clearly relevant to a psychologist interested, as Erikson was, in integration and the ego. Identity is the integration of integrations and, in that sense, can be regarded as the epitome of ego functioning. His experi-ences with American Indians, with adolescents and war veterans all confirmed his view that identity is a vital basis of psychological well-being. Most importantly, it is a topic of deep personal relevance for himself because of the complex roots of his own identity – an aspect we noted in Chapter 2 and will explore further in the final chapter.

Identity is experienced as a 'subjective sense of an invigorating sameness and continuity'.[6] Erikson quotes as descriptive of this experience of identity a passage from a letter which William James wrote to his wife (although James uses the term 'character' in place of identity).

A man's character is discernible in the mental or moral attitude in which, when it came upon him, he felt himself most deeply and intensely active and alive. At such moments there is a voice inside which speaks and says: '*This* is the real me!'[7]

In part, identity rests on a synthesis of all the different selves we experience.

There are constant and often shocklike transitions between these selves: consider the nude body self in the dark or suddenly exposed in the light; consider the clothed self among friends or in the company of higher-ups or lower-downs; consider the just awakened drowsy self or the one stepping refreshed out of the surf or the one overcome by retching and fainting; the body self in sexual excitement or in a rage; the competent self and the impotent one; the one on horseback, the one in the dentist's chair, and the one chained and tortured – by men who also say 'I'. It takes, indeed, a healthy personality for the 'I' to be able to speak out of all of these conditions in such a way that at any given moment it can testify to a reasonably coherent Self.[8]

The experience of a continuity of self and that other people recognize it, fosters a sense of *personal identity*. But what Erikson calls *ego identity* is more than this. He is reluctant to risk emasculating this concept by defining it but it involves process as well as an awareness of the self. Perhaps the nearest he gets to a definition is:

From a genetic point of view, then, the process of identity formation emerges as an evolving configuration – a configuration which is gradually established by successive ego resyntheses throughout childhood. It is a configuration gradually integrating constitutional givens, idiosyncratic libidinal needs, favoured capacities, significant identifications, effective defenses, successful sublimations and consistent roles.[9]

This is something of a mouthful but if taken step by step and bearing in mind his conceptions of triple book-keeping, ego development and the life cycle discussed in the previous chapters, it clearly conveys a kind of superordinate individual synthesis of the more specific integrations the ego is required to make through life.

Erikson conceives of identity as *psychosocial*. 'We deal with a process "located" *in the core of the individual* and yet also *in the core of his communal culture'*.[10] The development of identity involves an individual's relationship with his cultural context. Effective assertion of identity requires recognition and response from others (even if these are only assumed) and a relation between some wider section of the society and the individual himself 'be that section the neighbourhood block, an anticipated occupational field, an association of kindred minds, or perhaps (as in the case of G.B. Shaw) the "mighty dead"'.[11] (The phrase refers to writers and others who may no longer be alive and yet can be related to through their writings.) Nations, subcultures and classes offer attitudes, symbols and historical figures to identify with, creating a powerful substratum of unconscious feelings about what is good or bad, and shaping in this way the identities constructed by their individual members. Even where membership of a tradition or culture is nominally rejected, it may still cast its spell. Although Freud as an adult never professed or practised his Jewish faith, he still acknowledged its influence on his 'inner identity' and the independence and clarity of mind which this fostered in the face of majority resistance to his ideas. The intrinsically psychosocial nature of identity, Erikson argues, means that it can only be studied effectively if viewed both from the perspectives of society *and* individual personality, each in relation to the other.

In summary, Erikson's use of the term *identity* tends to cover four primary aspects of personality – 'a conscious *sense of individual identity;* ... an unconscious striving for a *continuity of personal character,* ... the silent doings of *ego synthesis;* and ..... an inner *solidarity* with a group's ideals and identity'.[12] In his view, identity is never finally 'established' as an 'achievement' but is dynamic and evolves during the course of a person's lifetime both through direct experience of oneself and the world and through being aware of the way others react to you.

> ... in psychological terms, identity formation employs a process of simultaneous reflection and observation, a process taking place on all levels of mental functioning, by which the individual judges himself in comparison to themselves and to a typology significant to them; while he judges their way of judging him in the light of how he

perceives himself in comparison to them and to types that have become relevant to him. This process is, luckily, and necessarily, for the most part unconscious except where inner conditions and outer circumstances combine to aggravate a painful, or elated, 'identity-consciousness'.

Furthermore, the process described is always changing and developing: at its best it is a process of increasing differentiation and it becomes ever more inclusive as the individual grows aware of a widening circle of others significant to him, from the maternal person to 'mankind'. The process 'begins' somewhere in the first true 'meeting' of mother and baby as two persons who can touch and recognize each other, and it does not 'end' until a man's power of mutual affirmation wanes.[13]

The processes of identity development

In *Childhood and Society* Erikson discusses the processes which he considers to be involved in the evolution of identity. As we have seen, these include the integration of biological development and social influences in the growth of the ego and in children's play. To these he adds the child's need for recognition and figures with whom to identify, and the more conscious identity conflicts of adolescence. In subsequent writings[14] he elaborates on this. The development of identity rests in particular, he claims, on three processes – *introjection, identification* and *identity formation* 'by which the ego grows in ever more mature interplay with the available models'.[15] The basis is provided by the *introjections* of the infantile period; that is, when the young child internalizes the injunctions and demands of parents and other key figures and thus, as it were, establishes inner representations of them. This is further developed by the child, as he grows older, through *identifications* with people who assume significance in his life. In so doing, he or she adopts their characteristics and attitudes. But identity involves more than these. It evolves in a sequence of progressive differentiations – tentative and changing crystallizations of identity – as a result of introjection, identification and a child's growing awareness of his own powers and weaknesses and his place in the social context. The key process in Erikson's conceptualization of identity comes in adolescence when:

> *identity formation,* finally, begins where the usefulness of identification ends. It arises from the selective repudiation and mutual assimilation

of childhood identifications and their absorption in a new configuration, which, in turn, is dependent on the process by which a society (often through subsocieties) identifies the young individual, recognizing him as a somebody who had to become the way he is and who, being the way he is, is taken for granted.[16]

Identity formation involves expanding self-awareness and more conscious exploration of self. The critical period for this is *adolescence:*

that period of the life cycle when each youth must forge for himself some central perspective and direction, some working unity, out of the effective remnants of his childhood and the hopes of his anticipated adulthood; he must detect some meaningful resemblance between what he has come to see in himself and what his sharpened awareness tells him others judge and expect him to be.[17]

Adolescence and choice

Adolescence becomes a time of choice – choice of occupation, life style, values and ways of relating to others. Choices made both influence and reflect the shifting phases of evolving identity. As we noted in the previous chapter in discussing the identity stage, Erikson argues that the phenomena of adolescence essentially express these processes of identity formation and exploration.

In general it is the inability to settle on an occupational identity which most disturbs young people. To keep themselves together they temporarily overidentify with the heroes of cliques and crowds to the point of an apparently complete loss of individuality. Yet in this stage not even 'falling in love' is entirely, or even primarily, a sexual matter. To a considerable extent adolescent love is an attempt to arrive at a definition of one's identity by projecting one's diffused self-image on another and by seeing it thus reflected and gradually clarified. This is why so much of young love is conversation. On the other hand, clarification can also be sought by destructive means. Young people can become remarkably clannish, intolerant, and cruel in their exclusion of others who are 'different', in skin color or cultural background, in tastes and gifts, and often in entirely petty aspects of dress and gesture arbitrarily selected as the signs of an in-grouper or out-grouper. It is important to understand in principle (which does not mean to condone in all of its manifestations) that such intolerance may be, for a while, a necessary defense against a sense of identity loss. This is unavoidable at a time of life when the body changes its proportions radically, when genital puberty floods body and imagination with all manner of impulses, when intimacy with the other sex approaches and is, on occasion, forced on the young person, when the immediate future confronts one with too many conflicting possibilities and choices. Adolescents not only help one another temporarily through such discomfort by forming cliques and stereotyping themselves, their ideals, and their enemies; they also insistently test each other's capacity for sustaining loyalties in the midst of inevitable conflicts of values.[18]

Young people need something to believe in. In the search for identity, they experiment with ideas, actions and devotions. Erikson detects *polarities* in this process – a need for freedom and yet a capacity for discipline, a yearning for adventure and yet a love of tradition. There is too a concern both for individuality and being part of a group or community. Erikson sees the disco as a potent expression of this.

> ... songs of shouted loneliness underscored by a pounding rhythm-to-end-all-rhythms in a sea of circling colors and lights. Such active and joint mastery of a cacophonous world can be experienced with an emotional and physical abandon unlike anything the older generation has known; and yet – especially where compounded by drugs – it can also camouflage a reciprocal isolation of desperate depth.[19]

On one side there is total devotion to a principle or group, on the other a need for repudiation.

> In their late teens and early twenties, even when there is no explicit ideological commitment or even interest, young people offer devotion to individual leaders and to teams, to strenuous activities, and to difficult techniques; at the same time they show a sharp and intolerant readiness to discard and disavow people (including, at times, themselves).[20]

Negative identifications

Repudiation may be an important element in the development of identity. Erikson uses the term *negative identification* to refer to the process of disdaining or rejecting roles preferred by family or immediate community as desirable. It may take the form of a direct reaction to the image of their parents. So if a father is a businessman or academic, that is the last thing his son or daughter will want to be. Erikson also uses negative identification in a somewhat different sense to indicate identification with people, ideas or life-styles which are *not* valued by family and other 'establishment' adults, or which are considered by them to be dangerous or unsuitable. This may constitute a natural self-assertion in response to feelings of being overwhelmed by parental influence. It may even be unwittingly encouraged by the parents themselves.

> A mother who was filled with unconscious ambivalence toward a brother who had disintegrated into alcoholism again and again responded selectively only to those traits in her son which seemed to point to a repetition of her brother's fate, with the result that this 'negative' identity sometimes seemed to have more reality for the son than all his natural attempts at being good. He worked hard at becoming a drunkard, and, lacking the necessary ingredients, ended up in a state of stubborn paralysis of choice.[21]

Negative identification in both senses can operate in relation to cultural background as, for example, when someone aspires to move outside their class and in so doing rejects all that it stands for, or when a person comes to hold in contempt that which is typical of their own country and prizes only that which is foreign.

Identity then is in large part *relational*, that is, it is conceived in terms of comparison with others – with those we are like as well as those we are quite definitely *not*. Developing a coherent identity requires repudiation as well as identification, as when we make clear what we will never become or reject what we once were. This may mean the need for checks and inhibitions against which to assert ourselves. As Erikson puts it: 'where man does not have enemies he often must invent them in order to create boundaries against which he can assert the leeway of the new man he must become'.[22]

The aspects or potential aspects of ourselves which, in developing a coherent identity, we come to reject, William James has called our 'abandoned' or 'murdered' selves and Jung the 'shadow'. Erikson describes them as our *negative identity*. (Note though that he uses this term in several senses – for example, as above to indicate an identity based on defiant alignment with the culturally rejected and also, as we shall see later, an identity which is normally developed within a minority group but is regarded by the majority culture in a pejorative way.) Like Jung, he believes that such negative identities lurk in our unconscious, occasionally intruding into dreams, fantasies and behaviour. This is part of the reason why those who are perceived as fundamentally different to us may easily threaten our sense of identity and so generate aggressive, even violent reactions in its defence. When I interviewed Erikson for a BBC radio programme, he expressed it this way:

> Everybody carries around a self that he had to repress, suppress, which remains very important in later life because that is the one one usually then projects on an out-group. That is why one is ready to hate later. And why people under certain given ideologies so easily assume that another kind of man is wicked and one should fight that other, that other kind, go to war, or otherwise suppress him.[23]

The need for a 'psychosocial moratorium'

The process of exploration involved in identity formation requires time. If during that time *identity confusion* is severe, then life seems to happen 'to the individual rather than being lived by his initiative'.[24] Biff's cry in Arthur Miller's play *Death of a Salesman*, 'I just can't take hold, Mom, I can't take hold of some kind of a life' is to Erikson a cry expressive of identity confusion. It may also show itself in distant or aggressive moodiness or suddenly throwing up a job or course. The period between the end of childhood and the adoption of a coherent identity and acceptance of commitment Erikson refers to as a *psychosocial moratorium*. There is great individual variation in the length of this period. Erikson has argued that it is particularly inclined to be pronounced in very gifted people ('gifted for better or for worse' as he wryly adds). Not until Freud was 30 did he finally take up the work with patients that was to lead to his formulation of psychoanalysis. Darwin spent a period as an unsuccessful and somewhat dilettante student of medicine, before embarking, almost by chance, on the voyage on the Beagle which was to stimulate the work and ideas which came to dominate his life. Culture, Erikson points out, often institutionalizes this psychosocial moratorium. In the past, it may have been time spent in a monastery; for the wealthy of the nineteenth century, a grand European tour. In our contemporary society, it may take a variety of forms – from higher education, a period spent drifting or travelling, to delinquency or even the role of mental patient. The benefits from such moratoria come from the space they provide to resist consolidating particular roles and identity and to allow experimentation with the different possibilities a person may become.

Identity crisis

Adolescence is inevitably and normally a time of crisis for identity. How far this is disruptive will vary depending on individuals and their contexts. But Erikson believes that a degree of identity confusion is to be desired and that, even in later life, 'to have the courage of one's diversity is a sign of wholeness in individuals ...'[25] Problems may arise not just from a sense of unresolved confusion but also from making too firm a commitment too early. It is possible for a person to settle into an identity only to experience in later life a sense of *'identity crisis'* – a sudden awareness of one's own identity and its inadequacy or unsatisfying quality. Such a crisis may come about as a result of trauma or change in external circumstances which undermine the sense of identity already established – this is what happened in the case of the marine, described earlier in Chapter 2, who broke down during enemy bombardment. Or it may come about as part of the normal process of maturation as, for example, in the so-called 'mid-life crisis', the common tendency of people in our culture to engage during middle age in an intense review of the past and future patterns of their lives. An identity crisis may generate initial confusion followed by attempts to explore new identities, new avenues in life or new ways of being. It is at times of identity crisis that we come to greater awareness of aspects of our identity which hitherto may have been unconscious or have escaped our notice.

> ... between the double prongs of vital inner need and inexorable outer demand, the as yet experimenting individual may become the victim of a transitory extreme identity consciousness, which is the common core of the many forms of 'self-consciousness' typical for youth. Where the processes of identity formation are prolonged (a factor which can bring creative gain), such preoccupation with the

'self image' also prevails. We are thus most aware of our identity when we are just about to gain it and when we (with that startle which motion pictures call a 'double take') are somewhat surprised to make its acquaintance; or again, when we are just about to enter a crisis and feel the encroachment of identity confusion.[26]

In the same passage, Erikson goes on to describe the optimal sense of identity which may emerge from crisis. This is

experienced merely as a sense of psychosocial well-being. Its most obvious concomitants are a feeling of being at home in one's body, a sense of 'knowing where one is going' and an inner assuredness of anticipated recognition from those who count.[27]

It brings in its wake an acceptance of one's self and others, and the feeling of having some meaningful place in the scheme of things. It has the value also of laying down a firm basis for further development – for going on to confront issues of intimacy and generativity.

The processes which Erikson suggests are involved in the development of identity are then *introjection* and early *identifications, identity formation,* and the *negative identifications* (in both senses of the term) typical of adolescence. Identity is most likely to emerge from a *crisis* stage in adolescence or in later life, during which *identity confusion* will be paramount. A *psychosocial moratorium* when social pressures are held off and there is opportunity for exploration of roles, feelings and ideas, will be beneficial to the fostering of an optimal sense of identity and is necessary if premature commitment is to be avoided.

In his teaching at Harvard, Erikson used appropriate films to illustrate his ideas. We have already noted the way Bergman's *Wild Strawberries* was drawn on as an illustration of the life cycle. To express the essence of a strong sense of identity, Erikson cited Albert Finney's character in Karel Reisz's 1960 film *Saturday Night and Sunday Morning.* Finney's character refused to conform for the life set out for him as a factory worker and which his friends and co-workers passively accepted. In contrast he was the rebel, asserting his individuality regardless of social pressures, drawing on strengths within himself. It was Erikson's comments on this film that brought home to Erikson's students what an identity crisis and its resolution really meant – and provided an understanding that remained with them in later years.[28]

Case studies of identity development – Shaw and James

Erikson brings life to this analysis with brief references to case histories from his clinical practice – particularly of individuals with severe identity confusion,[29] but more particularly by using his concepts to illuminate the autobiographical commentaries of G.B. Shaw and William James. As he points out, the autobiographies of self-perceptive people offer a rich source of information about the nature of identity and the processes involved in its development. He traces back the elements of Shaw's evolving identity – the 'snob', the 'noise maker', '*enfant terrible*' and 'outsider' – to his early life and relations in his family. At the age of 20 reacting to a premature and too successful commitment to a business occupation, Shaw entered on a self-created moratorium which involved leaving Ireland and his work and roots behind. During the next few years, he purposely shied away from any opportunities offered him, for 'behind the conviction that they could lead to nothing that I wanted, lay the unspoken fear that they might lead to something I did not want'.

Two important ingredients of identity, according to Erikson, are the 'habitual use of a dominant faculty elaborated in an occupation' and 'an intelligible theory of the processes of life'.[30] Shaw found the former in his writing and he was able to infuse this with the habit of hard work which he had acquired earlier, so much so that he became almost compulsive in his pursuit of his goal ('I work, as my father drank'). He found the latter – his ideology in the Fabian Socialist revival of the 1880s. This gave him not only a group identity but a formula for repudiation, in that it gave him an outlet to vent his indignation at the social evils inflicted upon the world. The different facets of Shaw's identity though were complex and only a kind of *tour de force* allowed him to integrate them all.

> … a deeper strangeness … has made me all my life a sojourner on this planet rather than a native of it. Whether it be that I was born mad or a little too sane, my kingdom was not of this world: I was at home only in the realm of my imagination, and at my ease only with the mighty dead. Therefore I had to become an actor, and create for myself a fantastic personality fit and apt for dealing with men, and adaptable to the various parts I had to play as author, journalist, orator, politician, committee man, man of the world, and so forth.[31]

Erikson's analysis of James' life may be sketched more briefly, but his debt to him is greater for James' theoretical writings and particularly his personal letters provided a rich source of thoughts about the nature of identity. James in his youth had faced what Erikson calls 'an "identity crisis" of honest and desperate depth'[32] which had led him over a period of years from art school to scientific studies and eventually to medicine; and from the USA to South America, to Europe and back again. James' life follows the creative pattern of late commitment. At 26, he was complaining of his desire 'for a constructive passion of some kind' and not till he was 30 did he begin his career as a university teacher. In middle age, under the stress of a heart complaint, came further crisis when he remembers 'wondering how other people could live, how I myself had ever lived, so unconscious of that pit of insecurity beneath the surface of life'. Erikson draws out the psychosocial aspects of James' identity problems, offering glancing insights as to their possible links with both his relationship with his father and family and with the wealthy middle-class background from which he came.

Identity and culture

We have already seen that identity has a strongly social aspect. The development of any individual identity is embedded in a culture. This offers a shared world image, particular sets of roles and ritualizations to initiate its members into its institutions and ways of life, values to act as arbiters of what is good and evil, and images and symbols to act as guides in the enterprise of living. Thus, according to Erikson, 'true identity ... depends on the support which the young individual receives from the collective sense of identity characterizing the social groups significant to him: his class, his nation, his culture'.[33] To understand any person's identity then requires us to know something about the social and historical context in which they live.

But the concept of identity can be applied to societies themselves. In Erikson's comparison of the nomadic Sioux with the settled Yurok, he showed us how the fabric of a culture can form a coherent pattern. The identity configuration of a complex industrial society is likely to be fragmented and confused, and analysing it an even more speculative venture, but in *Childhood and Society* Erikson tries his hand when he considers the kinds of problem young people in post-war America, pre-war Germany and pre-revolutionary Russia confronted in developing their identities. Although always open to question, Erikson's analyses are rich, imaginative and,

I think, full of interesting insights. He draws on literature, myth and folksong to pick out key images and themes. While he focuses on family structure and the relationship of the growing child to his parents, he is also sensitive to the significance of historical background, ecology and economics – the part played in the shaping of any society by its origins, geographical context and means of survival.

American identity

Although the identity configuration of North American society was first explored by Erikson in *Childhood and Society* (1950),[34] this was subsequently supplemented by an essay in *Toys and Reasons* (1977)[35] on its collective visions and nightmares. His approach to coping with the complicated network of subcultures, roles and styles of life which any modern society must represent, is to focus selectively on some of its core features and images. One critical aspect of American society, for example, is what he regards as its essentially *adolescent* nature. By this, he means that there is a pervasive openness about identity, a refusal to be pinned down or committed, a continual search for new roles and experiences and a strong belief in the notion of the 'self-made', person – that we all have the freedom to create who we are. If we accept Erikson's suggestion here that wherever cultures become 'Americanized', people become more concerned about issues of identity, this must raise questions as to how far his own emphasis on and analysis of identity is culture-bound.

A second core ingredient of American identity Erikson suggests is *puritanism,* expressed in both a powerful work ethic and the sense of a search for a lost paradise which can only be restored through arduous effort.

Most of the features he ascribes to American identity are conceived as a series of *polarities* or oppositional characteristics. So while there is a strong sense of individuality, at the same time there is a tendency towards conformity; originality is prized and yet standardization abounds. It is a country which could prosecute with vigour the Vietnam War and yet be appalled at the atrocities committed there. At once internationalist yet isolationist, it encompasses ethnic groups who jealously guard their traditions while aspiring to an American citizenship common to all. It represents the most complex mix of nationalities the world has probably ever known and yet reveals often surprising ignorance about the rest of the world. (This last point was brought home to me during a recent spell teaching at an eminent Californian University. An undergraduate asked me, after several weeks of lectures, where I came from. On being told England, he politely enquired how it was then that I could speak English so well!) Overt dynamic polarities which Erikson adds are 'migratory and sedentary, individualistic and standardized, competitive and cooperative, pious and free thinking, responsible and cynical ...'[36]

Erikson was familiar with the notion of polarities from his schooldays. He had encountered them in reading Goethe and from discussions with the father of his schoolmate Peter Blos. He had even used them in his poems and writings during his years spent wandering after leaving school. Such polarities are not unique to America. Erikson believed they typify every complex society and give each its unique style, undermining its coherence only when the self-contradictions they represent become extreme.

Drawing on his experience of American patients as well as popular song, myth and history, he goes on to construct a series of *key images*. These are sketched with a few bold lines but are saved from caricature by the subtlety of his shading. Emphatically art rather than photography, they are very much a personal view. They offer a rich array of seemingly potentially powerful insights but no way of checking their validity.

The first image he explores is that of '*Mom*' – the traditional American mother. He sees her in stereotype as dominating the family and sexually rejecting towards her spouse. Rather than fostering warmth and sensuality, she is eager to encourage independence in her children and this can leave them with a sense of having been abandoned. The source of such a pattern he attributes to unconscious adjustment to women's historical role in frontier society. There she was often the sole provider of education and culture as well as fulfilling the traditional tasks of motherhood. Only by being autocratic could she hope to impose any kind of civilized and settled life on unruly menfolk resistant to being tied down. Ensuring that her children could cope for themselves could well be vital to their survival.

Another portrait is of that classic symbol of American identity – the *cowboy*. Again there is the fear of emotion and sensuality. In cowboy songs love becomes something to run away from or to laugh at. Endurance and audacity are what count. But again polarities are evident. The cowboy's callous indifference to the cattle in his charge is countered by the tenderness of the lullabies he sings to them on their journey. He is cautious of commitment and stays endlessly on the move and yet he dreams too of settling down in some misty and improbable future. Erikson points to the power of such images for contemporary Americans and how they are reflected in their behaviour – more people in America for example, move residence and spend their retirement travelling than in any other modern society.

Erikson is concerned not just with the characteristics of American identity but with explaining why they take the form they do. As with his studies of the Sioux and Yurok, he views the culture in terms of its historical origins and the economic and geographical bases of its way of life. One significant factor he emphasizes, as we have seen, is its history as a *frontier* society. He considers that this is the source of the polarization between sedentary and migratory life styles. A decision always had to be made as to whether to settle down or move on and it had to be asserted vigorously in order to counteract the influence of those doing otherwise. But whichever was chosen, a feeling was always left in the recesses of the mind that the other may have been the better course. From frontier life too come the values of autonomy and self-reliance and a fear of being too old to choose or act.

Another great historical factor has been industrialization. As the buffalo was to the Sioux, and the salmon to the Yurok, so, Erikson considers, the *machine* is a key to modern American identity. The values of a machine age – efficiency, standardization and conformity – come to overlay those of frontier society, this fusion itself generating polarities. There are polarities which are also intrinsic to machine culture; for example, the power it confers does not redeem the feelings of powerlessness it provokes – 'the sense that modern life made all too many people aimless and voiceless robots in a blueprint without boundaries'.[37]

It is important to understand not just the origins of the pattern of cultural identity but also how it comes to be maintained. As in his studies of Indian tribes, Erikson believes the key to this lies in the experiences of childhood and family life. He comments on the implications of the small size of the typical American family and the careful toilet training. The aim is, he considers, to create 'the machine ideal of functioning without friction'. The problem is that the controls this demands can undermine another value – the need for autonomy and exerting free choice. The stimulation of resentment is avoided though by an initial tolerance with children which lays a basis for later co-operation. Erikson focuses his account on the typical American male adolescent – his relations with parents, his activities and attitudes and what he values, hopes for and fears. Erikson notes, for example, the disregard for feelings and the intellect, and how sport comes to substitute for sensual experience. He also articulates with delicate skill the subtle ambivalence that characterizes American father-son relations, and how an almost fraternal relationship of joking can provide a way of avoiding overt conflict.

Erikson's portrait of American identity of the immediately post-war period is a marvellously vivid and detailed set of interrelated sketches, full of wise reflections and seemingly penetrating insights. But it is speculative. While it remains a rich source of ideas, questions and hypotheses, as there are no immediate means of assessing its validity, it should only be taken with circumspection and several grains of salt.

German and Russian identities

The two other portraits of industrial societies he presents are of Germany between the Wars[38] and Russia at the turn of the century. Understandably, Erikson was interested in the man who had been ultimately responsible for his more-or-less enforced emigration to the New World. But he realizes that Hitler could not have achieved such power had he not appealed to core aspects of *German identity*. To analyse the nature of this appeal, he works from Hitler's account of his life in the early chapters of *Mein Kampf*. Not that he accepts this at face value. He takes it as a myth, but one which is of interest because of the power it had to evoke a ready response from large sections of the German population. Erikson's essay in *Childhood and Society* on this theme is the outcome of work he had begun before leaving Germany and which had been developed in his wartime analysis of Hitler's appeal to German youth.

Erikson sees Hitler's description of his relations with his mother and father as an idealized version of the strongly paternalistic and Oedipal pattern which he claims was commonly found among German families of the time. The growing German boy experienced much more intense ambivalence towards his father than his American equivalent, culminating in a more rebellious adolescence. By presenting himself in the image of a tough, adolescent, elder brother, a Führer not a Kaiser or President, Hitler was able to exploit this.

> He was the unbroken adolescent who had chosen a career apart from civilian happiness, mercantile tranquillity, and spiritual peace: a gang leader who kept the boys together by demanding their admiration, by

creating terror, and by shrewdly involving them in crimes from which there was no way back.[39]

Another feature of German identity which Erikson explores is a polarity which he ascribes to Germany's situation in the centre of Europe. On one hand there is a cosmopolitan delight in other cultures, on the other a fear and resentment of foreign influence. Had German society been confident and strong, a minority group in their midst like the Jews could have been accommodated and accepted as a source of vitality. As it was, with the German people anxious and disillusioned from their defeat in the First World War, it became a fear which Hitler could manipulate to his own advantage. Again we find the familiar ingredients in Erikson's analysis. A configuration of collective identity is sketched and then understood by reference to geographic and historical circumstances mediated by family structure: '... historical and geographic reality amplify familiar patterns and ... in turn, these patterns influence a people's interpretation of reality'.[40] It is worth emphasizing Erikson's recognition of the complexity of such issues. He refuses, for example, to make trite and obvious interpretations about Hitler's personality and his influence. There have been articles in psychoanalytic literature which claim such simple causality. But it obviously takes much more than an individual complex to make a successful revolutionary.[41]

As he was to do later with Bergman's *Wild Strawberries*, Erikson focuses his essay on *Russian identity* on the analysis of a film – in this case an old Soviet one on the legend of Maxim Gorky's youth. This is supplemented by reading from Russian history and Gorky's own work. Working from a detailed narrative of the film, Erikson's approach is again to depict a series of vivid images and to explore their implications in the light of Russian history, geography and the conditions under which the majority of the population were forced to live.

We are made aware of polarities – the prevalence of warm and benevolent mother images contrasting with the hard cruelty of older males. The practice of swaddling babies – binding their limbs tightly and unwrapping them only occasionally for moments of free release – is seen as a parallel to the pattern of hard work and atonement interspersed by brief spells of manic indulgence, like the cycle of long winters followed by summer. Why, Erikson wonders is there a tendency throughout Russian history to passively accept control by others, be these foreign invaders or their own so often cruel rulers? He attributes this partly to an 'inner serfdom' – an unconscious sense of primal guilt and moral weakness. The tragic excesses of a despot could serve a 'collective ego function', playing out for the people their own repressed needs and desires for atonement and revenge.

In contrast with Americans, we find an emphasis in the Russian character not on immediate action but on *caution*. Erikson writes of the dominance of the *eye* – quiet observation, learning to resist temptation, having understanding and a clear vision of the way ahead before making any decisive move. If this analysis of Russian identity seems more discursive, less systematized even than the other two, it still leaves the reader with a strong impression, if perhaps a partial and sometimes questionable one, of the pattern of Russia's traditional culture and the roots of her identity.

'Pseudospeciation' and other problems of cultural identity

If the identity of a society emerges from political, historical and environmental circumstances, it is also given life by the unconscious needs and projections of its members. Childhood experience provides a basis which politicians, religions and social institutions can all too easily exploit – an exploitation which Erikson believes must be devoutly resisted.

Like individuals, societies too can experience *crises of identity*. These may arise because new technologies and changing social and political structures or extensive immigration may disrupt an established equilibrium, arousing anxieties about the erosion of traditional values and ways of doing things. Or increasing complexity and secularization may result in an identity confusion or underlying 'existential dread' because they undermine the likelihood of shared goals and beliefs. Paradoxically though, the imposition of too consolidated an identity may also provoke crisis. As it did in Hitler's Germany, it may lead to lack of flexibility and squeeze out the variety upon which the vitality of a society depends. Or where such consciously imposed identity depends on setting up a 'negative identity' against which to react – as Hitler used the Jews and some contemporary Islamic regimes invoke a demonology embracing both Western materialists and Marxists – then crisis is likely to ensue because of the eventual conflict and instability this may well precipitate.

Erikson has pointed out how ritualizations – 'the formalisation of minute patterns of daily interplay', the ways we say 'hello', dress, eat our food and so on – inevitably tend to foster a sense of corporate identity within a group or culture. The power of ritualizations to do this is illustrated by the way any imposed change of them – for example, when Falkland Islanders were required to drive on the right by the Argentine invaders instead of on their customary left – comes to be regarded as an assault on identity. This tendency to corporate identity in the past has been adaptive, leading to a variety of artistic and technological achievements because of devotion to religion or community. But such solidarity can all too easily foster what Erikson called '*pseudospeciation*'. Erikson initially put forward this idea in a paper to the Royal Society in 1966. Each group or tribe tends to regard itself as central – as *the* human species – considering most, if not all, others as 'a freakish and gratuitous invention of some irrelevant deity'.[42] The social institutions and, in particular, the ideology of a culture or group usually support and encourage this notion. Other groups may be used as a convenient screen on which to project negative identifications – the 'necessary, if most uncomfortable counterparts' of the identities assumed. Thus, if we are chosen, they are not; if we are good, they are evil; if we are cool, they are straight or square. The danger is that in-group feeling tends to carry with it a disdain or even hatred of those outside the circle. Unscrupulous politicians have been known to try to stimulate this as a way of increasing unity of feeling in their own country. The hostility and bloody conflict that pseudospeciation can provoke between nations now, especially with the development of nuclear arms, threatens the well-being and survival of us all. Fortunately, Erikson believed, humans are malleable in this respect. Throughout history, smaller groupings have been melded into larger ones and have come to share their values and develop a common identity. To counteract pseudospeciation we must work harder at this, moving towards a universal identity embracing all humankind.

The tendency to pseudospeciation operates also within a nation – in the different subcultures, castes and classes of which it is comprised. As the history of Northern Ireland (to take but one of many examples) can testify, it is a problem which becomes particularly acute when a minority culture is encapsulated rather than integrated within a larger one. Not only is the likelihood of serious conflict increased but there may well be a clash between two rather different versions of human existence, in which the dominant culture may succeed in imposing the view that the identity of the minority group is in some way inferior. (Erikson calls this a 'negative identity' using the term in a rather different way than when this was discussed earlier in this chapter.) Such a process was seen at work with the Sioux.

> In the remnants of the Sioux Indians' identity, the prehistoric past is a powerful psychological reality. The conquered tribe has never ceased to behave as if guided by a life plan consisting of passive resistance to a present which fails to reintegrate the identity remnants of the economic past; and of dreams of restoration in which the future would lead back into the past, time would again become ahistoric, hunting grounds unlimited, and the buffalo supply inexhaustible – a restoration which would permit again the boundlessly centrifugal life of hunting nomads. Their federal educators, on the other hand, preach values with centripetal and localized goals: homestead, fireplace, bank account – all of which received their meaning from a life plan in which the past is overcome and in which the full measure of fulfilment in the present is sacrificed to an ever-higher standard of living in the future. The road to this future is not outer restoration but inner reform ...
>
> No wonder that Indian children, forced to live by both these plans, often seem blocked in their expectations and paralysed in their ambitions. For the growing child must derive a vitalizing sense of reality from the awareness that his individual way of mastering experience, his ego synthesis, is a successful variant of group identity and is in accord with its space time and life plan.[43]

Erikson has also looked at the identity problems faced by a black person in the USA. Here again he also argues there is a fundamental conflict between the identity models the child is exposed to. I think the force of Erikson's analysis is revealed by some of the powerful autobiographic material subsequently available which describes what it is like to be black in a predominantly white culture by, among others, James Baldwin[44] and Eldridge Cleaver.[45] In the *Autobiography of Malcolm* X,[46] for example, Malcolm describes the painful process of 'conking' – straightening the hair by the application of lye – in order to conform as far as possible to the stereotype of white appearance. Could I suggest that the mix of the two identities may be reflected also in black music? For, while major and minor modes are almost always kept strictly separate in music of European origin, in jazz they are, for the first time in any music style, consistently fused to form the 'jazz chord'.

In his writings on *female identity* Erikson seems to suggest that a similar process may operate for women as well. There is a tendency for their roles to be defined and evaluated in relation to the values and aspirations of men rather than in terms of their own intrinsic potentials and needs. In all such cases, Erikson implies, it is important to resist vigorously definition by others. Only through a true integration of diversity rather than by imposed subordination to one group's world-view, can societies move towards a wider identity embracing 'an all-human consciousness'.

Erikson recognized the formidable difficulties in the way of any study of cultural identity and acknowledges the sketchy nature of his own attempt. His analyses were not intended as definitive but to draw attention to two main themes. One, as we have seen above, is the problem of *pseudospeciation* and the need to work towards a more inclusive human identity. The other is to explore further the *complex interplay between individual and society*. People must be rooted in a society of some kind. The danger comes from the extremes of isolation or swamping conformity. Erikson's ideal is a dynamic balance between the two, a 'workable' psychosocial equilibrium. To understand this demands historical as well as psychological analyses. So whereas repression and Oedipal conflict may be of primary significance to people in a paternalistic society, the problem of identity may assume greater significance in a culture subject to deep-rooted and rapid change. Psychologists too often ignore, he felt, the significance of cultural context in determining the characteristics of people. Conversely, historians, Erikson claimed, too often neglect psychological factors, in particular the significance of childhood – 'the fateful dawn of individual consciousness', and the formative identity phase of youth. He concluded that psychology and history must come to work more closely in harness – a prescription he himself was to follow in the biographical studies of Luther and Gandhi which we shall consider in the next chapter.

6 Psychobiographical Studies

With his interests in the case histories of patients, in identity, development through life and the totality of the person, it is not surprising that Erikson's attention turned to the problems of *biography*. How can the flow and essence of a person's life be captured and reconstructed? How can the concepts and approach of psychoanalysis be brought to bear to illuminate it? We have already noted his partial attempts at doing this in his essays on aspects of the lives of *Shaw* and *James*.

Erikson wrote other biographical essays. In one controversial paper, Erikson reinterpreted a dream which Freud reported, seeing in it a reflection of Freud's existential situation and own crisis of identity at the time. (This was refused by the *International Journal of Psychoanalysis* after opposition from Anna Freud among others who regarded Erikson's methods as departing too far from the orthodoxy of Freudian analysis. It was eventually published in revised form in the *Journal of the American Psychoanalytic Association*).[1] Erikson further explored Freud's middle and most creative years in a lengthy book review on the publication of an English translation of Freud's correspondence with his friend and mentor Wilhelm Fliess.[2] His most rounded study of *Freud* came in the invited address he delivered at the University of Frankfurt on the occasion of Freud's birthday.[3] In this he not only detailed Freud's achievements as well as inner conflicts but drew a contrast between Freud and *Darwin* and briefly commented on the pattern of the latter's life. Among the lectures included in *Toys and Reasons*[4] is one on *Einstein*, though admittedly this is more a reflection on the physicist's approach and the significance of play for creative thought than any kind of biographical study. (Although Erikson never made this point himself, there are interesting resemblances (albeit superficial) between himself and the physicist. Not only was there some similarity in their appearance but both had a flair for playing with polarities and both recognized the relativity of perspectives as well as the significance of emotional life in any attempt to make sense of the world.)

Of course, Erikson was by no means the first to apply the tools of psycho-analysis to biography. The most eminent precursor was *Freud's own study of Leonardo*.[5] While this has been criticized on both factual and logical grounds,[6] it remains a subtle and imaginative study, in comparison to which many subsequent attempts by others to apply psychoanalytic insights to biography seem crass and mechanistic. Erikson's work in this area not only matched the elegance and sensitivity of Freud but operated from a broader base.

As we saw in his essay on Hitler's Germany, Erikson's particular interest was to *explore the relation between persons in history and the reasons why they came to exert the influence they did*. This came out too in passing references which he made in his writings to *Simon Bolivar*, the nineteenth century 'Liberator' of South America. His two detailed studies in *psychohistory* – his books on Luther and Gandhi – are set in very different places and periods and are almost as much studies of the social contexts of the time as they are of the protagonists.

Another factor which renders Erikson's approach very different from standard 'psychologizing' is the range of concepts he was able to bring to bear. These include not just those from orthodox psychoanalysis but his own ideas about ego development and identity which have been discussed in the preceding chapters. While Erikson did not shrink from the bold guess and imaginative reconstruction, he was also aware of the *method-ological problems* involved in enterprises of this kind – that facts are often few and questionable; also that both evidence and interpretation inevitably depend on the perspective of the investigator. This important notion of *relativity* (i.e., that any event or person can be assessed only from a partic-ular perspective which in itself must affect the assessment made) must be borne in mind when appraising *any* historical analysis. This is particularly true of those which, as his do, seek to make sense of the meanings below the surface of actions and events.

Martin Luther

Erikson's decision to study Martin Luther emerged out of his interest in identity. His book, subtitled *a study in psychoanalysis and history*, had its origins in the 1950s when he was working at the Austen Riggs Center in Stockbridge. Many of his patients there were young people who seemed to be struggling with issues of identity. He noted one young man in particular who had previously been studying to be a priest. Erikson's initial intention was to write up some of these patients as clinical studies of identity crises. However, stimulated also by a growing interest in religion, his project developed instead into a book on Luther. Erikson took a year off in 1957 and went with Joan to Mexico to write. Erikson was not a historian – his use of original documents was inevitably restricted and he was sometimes inclined to move imaginatively beyond whatever evidence there might be. His goal, however, was not so much to write a comprehensive history of Luther but to present him as a case study of a youth going through an identity crisis and finding his own 'voice'. Several distinguished academic friends, including the social scientist David Riesman and the psychologist Gardner Murphy provided helpful comments on drafts of the manuscript.

The major part of the book is focused on the earlier phases of Luther's life (i.e., from childhood to mid-thirties) which Erikson regarded as a splendid demonstration of an *extended crisis of identity*. His interest was to explore how Luther managed to resolve the inner conflicts tormenting him, his ego turning them to creative advantage by rendering them into the emotional power-base of his theology, and how that came to fire the imagination of his time. In other words, his task was not to reduce Luther to a diagnostic category but rather to understand the *'logic'* of his inner life, his 'working gifts' and his impact on society.

Erikson based his analysis on material from a wide range of sources. If there are relatively few agreed facts about the personal side of Luther's life, there were his own writings and more recently discovered personal notes, reported comments collected by his students and followers and a host of treatises by academics. In reviewing some of the latter, Erikson points out how each is presented from one perspective which may have some truth in it but which is often used to refute and exclude the others. None works with a theory which, like psychoanalysis, is broad enough to encompass and interrelate all the relevant factors – personal, religious and social – which bear on Luther's life. He is critical though of the one psychoanalytic-type study he does come across, complaining that psychoanalytic notions stick like a 'foreign body' in the thinking of the writer.

Erikson's own approach is vivid, impressionistic and indirect. His style is elegant and decorated with wry humour (speaking of Luther's partiality for pig parables, for example, he writes 'his colourful earthiness sometimes turned into plain porcography').[7] But it occasionally takes on a Germanic-like complexity which makes it not always easy to absorb. The effect of the whole is rather like a rich fruit cake: it can be heavy going but offers a bountiful mix for the reader who is prepared to persevere. There is a strong emphasis on imaginative reconstruction from a few facts and even legends, set against knowledge of the times and assumptions from psychoanalytic theory. As with his earlier study of Hitler, Erikson does not eschew legend as a source of data because of what it conveys about Luther's impact on the consciousness of the time. His descriptions are often personalized and intense, as if Erikson is reporting the direct experience of seeing and hearing Luther. His achievement sometimes seems akin to the novelist rather than the sober biographer though it is grounded in a capacity for scholarship – as evidenced, for example, by his ability to point out common misconceptions based on mistranslations from Luther's German.

The reader is not presented with a clear-cut narrative of evidence. Erikson's primary theme is the identity of Luther and his influence on the ideology of the time:

> ... how young Martin, at the end of a sombre and harsh childhood, was precipitated into a severe identity crisis for which he sought delay and cure in the silence of the monastery; how being silent, he became 'possessed', how being possessed, he gradually learned to speak a new language, *his* language; how being able to speak, he not only talked himself out of the monastery, and much of his country out of the Roman Church, but also formulated for himself and for all of mankind a new kind of ethical and psychological awareness: and how, at the end, this awareness, too, was marred by a return of the demons, whoever they may have been.[8]

The story of Luther's life

As the book proceeds the main events of Luther's youth and early adult life emerge. The little that is known of his childhood is developed into a plausible account. He was born in 1483. Family life, Erikson asserts, was hard (though the evidence for this has been disputed by others, for example Stannard, 1980).[9] Young Martin's father, a local miner, seemed to have affection for his son but was a harsh disciplinarian. (This assumption was based on a reported statement by Luther that his father and mother had both beaten him on different occasions.) He was certainly ambitious for his son's worldly progress. At 17, Luther became a serious and successful student at the University of Erfurt though subject to the bouts of depression which remained with him all his life. After his graduation, so the legend goes, he was caught in a thunderstorm, suffered some kind of fit and at once determined to enter a monastery, much to the chagrin of his father who wanted him to become a lawyer. It was some time before Luther could confront him with his decision. At the age of 23 he celebrated his first mass, during which he reports suffering some kind of paroxysm of doubt and, at the ceremony afterwards, quarrelled with his father. Several years later, he made an uneventful administrative trip to Rome, then settled as professor and priest at the University of Wittenberg. After much pondering on theological issues and a 'revelation' which stimulated his reformulation of the relationship between the individual believer, the Church and God, he brought events to a head by nailing up his 95 theses protesting against the practice of 'selling' indulgences. He was banned by the Pope and responded by publicly burning the Papal Bull in question. He was subsequently required to attend before the Emperor at Worms. Later, while hiding for a short time, he translated the New Testament into German and wrote pamphlets on his views including one against celibacy. He married, had a son and took the now deserted monastery in which he had once been a monk, as his parsonage and home for his family. Having set the Reformation in train and become famous in doing so, he settled back into an occasionally gluttonous, sometimes reactionary and often depressed middle age.

On this frame Erikson hangs a whole series of fascinating digressions. We learn of the development of Christianity from the pristine simplicity of the Paulinian era through increasing organizational complexity to the papal bureaucracy of Luther's time, details of everyday monastic life, of the commercialism of relics and indulgences ('... the arms of his beloved St. Anne ... were displayed in a church separately from the rest of her bones ... the halves of the bodies of St. Peter and St. Paul ... had been weighed to prevent injustice to the church harbouring the other halves').[10] Erikson offers lucid accounts of the methods of biblical exegesis and the mixture of realism, nominalism and mysticism that constituted the religious ideology of the day. He speculates on the symbolism of the Eucharist and the nature of religion, suggesting that religious ceremonial, especially when reinforced by 'a collected genius of poetry and artistry', is akin to dream-life in its 'recuperative value' – after experiencing it our unconscious can awake refreshed. He comments too on the significance of the Renaissance, 'the ego revolution *par excellence* ... the restoration of ego vanity over super-ego righteousness',[11] the influence of which, Erikson believes, can be traced in Luther. There is a kaleidoscope of asides which make small but telling points – for example, '... sensible people manage to live relatively lusty and decent lives: as moral as they must be, as free as they may be, and as masterly as they can be. If we only knew it, this elusive arrangement *is* happiness'.[12] He comments on Luther's fatherly superior Staupitz, to whom he was inclined to attribute the source of some of his ideas, 'maybe he was merely that right person of whom one likes to believe or to remember that he said the right thing'.[13] We find too the gallery of familiar faces about whom, as we have seen, Erikson has written elsewhere – Darwin, Hitler, Shaw, Freud all put in appearances at various points.

Erikson draws interesting parallels between Luther 'the first Protestant at the end of an age of absolute faith', and Freud 'the first psychoanalyst at the end of the era of absolute reason'.[14] The search for personal authenticity and the roots of personal responsibility was central to them both. By engaging in intensive, introspective self-confrontation they developed a system of ideas designed to free others from the yoke in one case of an over-institutionalized Church, in the other of the irrational mind. Both suffered a father complex and both have been misconstrued by followers. Erikson also likens induction into the profession of psychoanalysis to monastic practice. Both demand ascetism and total personal involvement. They require commitment and taking emotional risks. There is a mistrust of surface appearances, and the principle that only after working through to one's own core is one in a position to help others do the same. They encompass too a similar mixture of creative and destructive spirits, 'thus psychoanalysis also has its monkhood, its monkishness and its monkery'.[15] And certain aspects of monastic life, Erikson suggests, have the quality of group therapy.

Psychoanalysing Luther

Through all this varied material shines Erikson's primary concern – to apply his concepts to illuminate the events and impact of Luther's life. His starting point is his imagined version of Luther's early life where he supplements the meagre evidence available with suppositions as to what must have happened on the basis of psychoanalytic theory in the light of later events. In other words, he could be accused of not being averse to creating material to fit with his analysis. He is not alone though in supposing a difficult relationship with a disciplinarian father and a consequent severe Oedipus complex.[16] Erikson proposes that many of Luther's later conflicts and the form of their ideological resolution hinged on the unconscious residue of this, that he was seeking in religion both what he could not and what he did find in his father. The image of a wrathful God which continually plagued him, and his difficulty in accepting the intercession of the Virgin Mary both have their emotional origins in his childhood experience, as did his ultimate theological resolution of reaching God through the symbolism of his Son's passion. His thanks to God was given as to a father and rival who was generous in suffering him to live at all. The unconscious hostility he felt was handled by being transferred to both the Devil and the Pope.

Another theme which cries out to any psychoanalyst at all worthy of his salt is the strongly *anal* quality which permeates Luther's life and work. If we take Erikson's word for it (though he does not tell us on what it is based) Luther was a lifelong sufferer from constipation and urine retention. There is no doubt that his conversation was peppered with anal references. 'I am like ripe shit' he is reported as saying, 'and the world is a gigantic arse-hole. We probably will let go of each other soon.' There is even a strong indication that one of Luther's major revelations may have come to him while sitting on the lavatory. Not surprising to the analyst is accompanying strong evidence of obsessive trends. One of his first reported remarks is a classic expression of this – 'the more you cleanse yourself, the dirtier you get'.[17] He scrupulously followed every detail of the exacting monastic regimen and compulsively confessed the most minor transgressions. Erikson argues that the pattern of Luther's rebellion reflects anal defiance – as Luther put it himself, his wind in Wittenberg could be smelled in Rome. He taunts the devil 'I have shit in the pants and you can hang them round your neck and wipe your mouth with it'. In support of the notion of a link between anality and rebelliousness, Erikson points to 'the significance of the choice of the buttocks as the preferred place for corporal punishment: a safe place physiologically, but emotionally potentially dangerous, since punishment aggravates the significance of this general area as a battlefield of parental and infantile wills'.[18]

The main line of interpretative action rests on Erikson's brand of ego psychology with its focus on *identity*. So Luther's time in the monastery is seen as offering him the haven of a *psychosocial moratorium*. (Erikson points out that entering a monastery was much more in the normal line of events and demanded less commitment than it would do nowadays.) Luther's intense struggle over identity reached several *crisis* points – the fit in the thunderstorm mentioned earlier, for example, and later a putative event in the choir of the monastery which Erikson makes much of where Luther was supposed to have fallen to the ground roaring repeatedly 'It's not me! I am *not!*' Perhaps, one suspects, Erikson focuses on this incident because in the way he interprets it, it fits in with his conceptions so well. At any rate, his reading of it is rather different from the traditional view that Luther had been possessed by demons. He lists the elements of the fit: 'physical paroxysm; a degree of unconsciousness; an automatic verbal utterance; a command to change the over-all direction of effort and aspiration; and a spiritual revelation, a flash of enlightenment, decisive and pervasive as a rebirth'.[19] He interprets the experience as 'the epileptoid paroxysm of ego-loss, the rage of denial of the identity which was to be discarded'. Luther's father had always claimed his 'conversion' had been possession by devils and Erikson sees the fact of his having the fit as unconsciously confirming for Luther his father's assertion even while his words ('I am not!') desperately denied this. To Erikson, such panics stemmed directly from young Luther's sense of identity confusion. He points to its typical manifestations – a tortured self-consciousness, a shying away from intimacy, his willingness to repudiate the world to devote himself totally to the search for a meaningful 'ideology'. (Erikson uses this word here to mean 'an unconscious tendency underlying religious and scientific as well as political thought: the tendency at a given time to make facts amenable to ideas, and ideas to facts, in order to create a world image convincing enough to support the collective and the individual sense of identity'.)[20]

Not until he was almost 30 did Luther begin to resolve his extended crisis. His hard-won sense of identity, according to Erikson, rested on the kind of foundations we would theoretically expect. There was, for example, a positive relationship with a helpful *mentor* – Dr Staupitz, who had the therapeutic knack of saying the right thing at the right time. A series of *negative identifications* – refusal to follow the career his father wanted for him, for example, or even that of 'dirty peasant' like his father's ancestors – culminated in the most formative repudiation of his career – his rejection of Rome. The most crucial element though was Luther's *search for an inner sense of meaning.* For the people of his time, religious dogma provided the ideological guidelines for a collective sense of identity. It was Luther's achievement to forge it to his own needs. 'Philosophical and theological concepts were to him only old baskets for new bread, the hot, crisp bread of original experience'.[21] The development of his theological thinking, revealed in his first lectures as Doctor of Theology in Wittenberg when he emphasized emotional sincerity and meaning what you do – the words of Christ rather than the institution of the Church – was intrinsically interwoven with the evolution of his personal sense of identity.

Erikson does not neglect the role of *social context* in his analysis. He points out how it was the institution of the Church and the roles and ritualizations it provided which channelled and gave meaning to Luther's personal conflicts and concerns: how his superstitiousness and his quasi-hallucinations and belief in devils, as well as the anal tone of his imagery, would have been quite in keeping with the mining community in which he grew up, dependent as it was on digging deep into the earth, where success or fatal disaster might seem to rest on the whim of fate. In keeping with his thesis of *triple book-keeping*, Erikson makes allowance too for possible effects of constitutional factors – how these might have predisposed Luther to depression, and how, later, ear disease and a resulting ringing in his ears may have aggravated his tendency to 'hear voices'. He also suggests that Luther's identity diffusion did not just rest upon his hypersensitive conscience but on the 'erotic irritability' resulting from the frustration of drive which the 'suicide' of monastic celibacy imposed.

We find Erikson's characteristic interest in *polarities* and the paradoxical nature of psychological life. Luther's scrupulous observance of confession was defiant by its very insistence on obedience to the rules. He was at once earthy and yet mystical, extrovert yet introspective, rebel yet reactionary. Like the typical rebel, he vacillated between dominance and submission. Another polarity lies in the fact that

> ... this potentially so passionate man found he could not feel at all, which is the final predicament of the compulsive character. That is, he could not *have* the feelings which he so desperately wanted to feel, while on occasion (as in the fit in the choir) feelings *had him* in the form of phobic terrors and ugly rage.[22]

Luther's life cycle

Towards the end of his book, Erikson draws earlier hints together and provides us with an account of Luther's development through the 'Eight Ages' of life. He assumes that little Martin's mother provided 'a font of basic trust' but that he

> ... was driven early out of the trust stage, out from 'under his mother's skirts', by a jealously ambitious father who tried to make him precociously independent from women, and sober and reliable in his work. He succeeded, but not without storing in the boy violent doubts of the father's justification and sincerity; a lifelong shame over the persisting gap between his own precocious conscience and his actual inner state; and a deep nostalgia for a situation of infantile trust. His theological solution – spiritual return to a faith which is there before all doubt, combined with a political submission to those who by necessity must wield the sword of secular law – seems to fit perfectly his need for compromise.[23]

The residue of shame and doubt fuelled, Erikson believes, Luther's vivid descriptions of these emotions in relation to God. He traces back Luther's lifelong sense of guilt to the Oedipus stage and 'the strong indications of an especially heavy interference by Hans Luder (his father) with Martin's attachment to his mother'.[24]

In the stage of industry *versus* inferiority, Martin developed a particular competence in literacy, the foundation of his later capacity to use the spoken and printed word as the means of revolutionary change. As we have already seen, Erikson believes that the concept of an extended identity crisis is a necessary basis for any understanding of Luther's achievement. Because of his vow of celibacy, 'concupiscence' tormented Luther for much of his youth and early manhood and it was only relatively late in life with his marriage, his children and his followers, that his needs for intimacy and generativity were worked through. Although the crisis of integrity *versus* despair may be 'last in the lives of ordinary men' it is 'a lifelong and chronic crisis in a *homo religiosus*' for 'the religionist's problem of individual identity' becomes 'the same as the problem of existential identity'.[25]

By the end of the book the reader has ringing and alive in her or his head a vivid portrait of Luther the man, albeit a reconstructed one. We feel his extraordinary mixture of intensity, introspection, passionate desire for authentic feeling, his superstition, earthiness, sensuality, his deep depressions and his compulsive yet defiant obedience. Above all, we feel the dominance of his vocal rebelliousness – 'one of those addicts and servants of the Word who never know what they are thinking until they hear themselves say it, and who never know how strongly they believe what they say until somebody objects'.[26]

The interweaving of personal and social

The core message of Erikson's analysis is to point to the *ontogenetic basis of historical and ideological change* – its roots in emotional life and childhood experience. Luther worked his personal crises through the medium of theology and the institution of the Church. Much of what is taken for granted now, represents his concerns made public property. Erikson's interest too is in how Luther's theological reformulations came to catch on. Others like Wycliffe before him had made similar protestations and put forward analogous ideas. But in Luther's case they had enormous impact. There were *economic* reasons for this: the delight of the German aristocracy and populace to give up paying the equivalent of taxes to Rome. There were *technological* ones, too, for the newly-invented printing press played a major role in disseminating Luther's ideas. Erikson strives to paint a picture not just of Luther himself but of the times in which he lived – both political and historical, for to understand his impact requires a fully *psychosocial* analysis. Only in that way can we see how he became

> ... the herald of the age which was in the making and is – or was – still our age: the age of literacy and enlightenment, of constitutional representation, and of the freely chosen contract; the age of the printed word which at least tried to say what it meant and to mean what it said, and provided identity through its very effort.[27]

While Freud may have been 'a moralist without even a moralising message',[28] in Erikson's work, as befits an artist-philosopher rather than a scientist, moral themes lie closer to the surface. He warns of the propensity of social institutions to exploit as well as respond to infantile fears – shame, doubt and guilt – and developmental needs for trust and identity. Not for nothing was the typical age of entry into the monastery of Luther's period (as also into the ideological movements of today) the late teens and early twenties – a time of heightened receptivity likely to ensure assimilation into the fold. In both the past and present, Church and State have often depended on infantile anxieties to encourage the obedience of their members. Erikson draws attention also to the need to be aware of the consequences of the way we bring up our children. In commenting on the caning and whipping of children in Luther's period, he points out that 'the majority of men have never invented the device of beating children into submission'. If today we beat them less than they did in Luther's time, 'we are still harrying them through this imperfect world … to climb, improve, advance, progress'.[29]

Limitations of Erikson's analysis

Some of the limitations of Erikson's study of Luther have already been alluded to. One problem lies in the paucity and quality of the available evidence. As Erikson himself points out, even Luther's own accounts seem subject to his tendency to exaggeration and retrospective dramatization. Much of the other material is hardly more than legend. Erikson's method is to make liberal use of inference and imaginative reconstruction. He had great ability (though some might think it a limitation) to read much in very little. This means that some of the themes and events which are central to his interpretation may quite possibly have little grounding in actuality. To take just two examples mentioned previously, the evidence of his father's harsh treatment rests primarily on a reported reference by Luther to a beating, and the story of the fit in the choir where Luther fell to the ground crying 'It isn't me!' is based on little more than hearsay. The value of this to Erikson (but of concern to the critical reader) was the considerable scope it gave him to create what he wanted to find. This possibility is made more likely by his reliance on theory to generate his reconstruction. So his suppositions about the nature of Martin's childhood in part spring from what he would expect to be the case on the basis of psychoanalytic propositions, in view of Luther's later character and actions. Quite apart from the circularity of this approach and the arguable validity of the propositions concerned, one might question how far they can be applied to a situation so far removed from the social context in which they were first formulated. Is there any reason to suppose, for example, that Erikson's 'Eight Ages' and the centrality of identity would have had the same currency in Luther's time as they might today?

Such limitations have led some writers to refer to *Young Man Luther* as a 'pyramid of conjectures'. Stannard[30] acknowledges Erikson's work as 'elegant and sensitive' and 'likely the best of the genre' but argues that problems of this kind are endemic in psychohistory because they are inevitable to the enterprise itself. While at its best psychohistory may offer 'insight, learning, sensitivity, and, most of all, imagination', virtually all works in the field suffer from the kind of problems of logic, fact, theory and cultural bias which have been indicated above.

The relatively few reviews of the book from historians, psychoanalysts and theologians were mixed. Anna Freud did not like it. Some historians praised the originality of its insights, but more criticized the lack of evidence to support its assertions. The book held most appeal for creative people who saw the significance of the portrayal of a man facing an identity crisis and finding his voice. Almost surely Erikson's analysis was the unacknowledged stimulus for the English playwright John Osborne's successful play on Luther.

Erikson clearly recognized the formidable difficulties his chosen approach involves. He points, for example, to the failure of psychoanalysis to deal adequately with the importance of work in the lives of people, and is dismissive of psychohistorical studies which are simple-mindedly deterministic. Many, if not most, of his own formulations are explicitly tentative – his book is full of statements of the 'it may be', 'seems to have', 'it is fair to assume' kind. But, like Freud, while he does sometimes acknowledge the hypothetical nature of an assertion he was not averse to using it at a later stage as if it were an established fact. Erikson acknowledges that there is much about his subject-matter that can never be directly known, but he remains optimistic about the ultimate value of psychohistory in spite of its imperfections.

> We may have to risk that bit of impurity which is inherent in the hyphen of the psycho-historical as well as of all other hyphenated approaches. They are the compost heap of today's interdisciplinary efforts, which may help to fertilize new fields, and to produce future flowers of new methodological clarity.[31]

Erikson's achievement

Erikson did not set out to present a comprehensive biography but to apply psychoanalytic insights to illuminate a central aspect of Luther's life – 'the transformation of a young man into a great one'. His account certainly serves to illustrate how his theoretical concepts can be applied. But it does much more than this. As Weinstein has pointed out, Erikson amply fulfilled the social function of intellectuals 'to provide the conceptual language people need to bring order to the complex experiences of everyday life'.[32] His book on Luther demonstrates the power of the psychoanalytic approach and its concepts to integrate a wide diversity of information and make sense of it. The outcome is a subtle, sensitive and plausible configuration of Luther's existence in the context of his time. But although this is no doubt a *tour de force,* it is of an artistic and philosophical kind rather than a scientific analysis. We are offered some criteria for assessing it – Erikson suggests, for example, that 'in biography, the validity of any relevant theme can only lie in its crucial recurrence in a man's development, and in its relevance to the balance sheet of his victories and defeats'.[33] But this is hardly a measure of a precise or reassuring kind. Nor does Erikson offer a method. Anyone who sought to emulate his example would be forced onto their own resources of skill and art without the guidance of an explicit technique.

But, Erikson would have asked, what other way *is* there to 'take a great man for what he was'? A biographer cannot avoid reconstruction and psychological interpretation of some kind though this may be hidden in the guise of 'common sense'. One might also question here the spurious nature of any approach which claims to be 'objective'. Any biography must view the subject from *some* perspective and rest on assumptions about people and life. What is important is that these should be made explicit. One great strength of a good psychoanalytic investigator is that he or she is prepared, as Erikson was, to turn his method on himself – to question his own bias, motivations, constructions and their origins. In place of objectivity Erikson emphasizes *empathy,* arguably a more realistic and effective basis for understanding another human being, even when that person lived over 400 years ago.

Mohandas Gandhi

Since his student days Erikson had admired Gandhi. Then, in 1962, he was invited to India to give a seminar on the life cycle. The invitation was extended by the nephew and children of Ambalal Sarabhai, the mill owner whom Gandhi had confronted in the 1918 strike which featured in his autobiography. They knew of Erikson through mutual friends who had introduced them to *Childhood and Society.* Joan and Erikson stayed in Ahmedabad for three months initially and then went back to India again in 1964. Although he did not venture much from the comfort and security of the Sarabhai residence, Erikson was fascinated by India and took what opportunity he could to collect information on Indian conceptions of the life cycle. On his return, he started work on a book on Gandhi. He himself was 62 years old. Erikson had a team of helpers for research and editing. These included Joan, his son Kai (now an academic himself), one of his teaching assistants from Harvard, Pamela Daniels and Sudhir Kakar, a relative of his hosts who tried to teach him about aspects of Indian culture.

Erikson's book *Gandhi's Truth: on the Origins of Militant Non-violence* did not appear until 1969.[34] Its publication was immediately preceded by a summary version in the form of an essay in *Daedalus* called 'On the nature of psychohistorical evidence'[35] which, as its title suggests, focused especially on methodological issues. The book itself centres on an event which took place in Ahmedabad in 1918 when Gandhi, who was 48 at the time, helped to organize a campaign of non-violent resistance in support of a strike of mill workers. Around this centrepiece is woven a complex of reflections on Indian society, on Gandhi's life and character, and on the particular brand of militant non-violence he perfected and its implications for humanity. The book is long, rambling and less focused than *Young Man Luther*, achieving its effect through the gradual accumulation of details and insights, leaving a residue of awareness rather like that which comes from experiencing a person or event in everyday life. In contrast to its predecessor, it is centred on a man in middle age.

Although a search for official documents and newspaper reports of the strike proved disappointing, Erikson, in this case, was not short of sources of information. Gandhi provided his own record of events in his autobiography *The Story of my Experiments with Truth* (1927).[36] There were several books on Gandhi including two biographies by people who had known him intimately. Erikson also made several subsequent visits to India to interview through interpreters several people who had known Gandhi at the time of the strike. These included his hosts' father – the now elderly mill owner Ambalal and his sister Anusaya Sarabhai who had taken Gandhi's and the mill workers' side.

Methodological problems of psychohistory

A major feature of the book is that it throws into relief the problems inherent in psychohistory and explicitly confronts the kind of issues which I raised earlier in commenting on the limitations of the Luther study. For example, how can the often conflicting reports of different witnesses be assessed? While variations in accounts of Gandhi can be in part attributed to the genius of any leader to 'elicit a variety of projections, each true, and yet none exclusively so',[37] they must also stem from differences in the perspectives of the witnesses themselves. Each reflects a particular relationship of an individual witness to the people and events being described. They also differ depending on the different roles and motives they ascribe to the interviewer, the dynamics of each of their individual personalities and the customary conceptual schemas through which they view the world.

There are other problems – the reticence of interviewees, ethical inhibitions about publishing material considered to be sensitive, the confounding of memories by the mythical image that Gandhi has come to represent. Gandhi's own reflections were *reinterpretations* of past events. They served the purpose, Erikson suggests, like any other autobiography, of 're-creating oneself in the image of one's method; and ... to make that image convincing'.[38] Even the fact of their translation from the Gujarati in which they were originally written makes it sometimes difficult to be certain whether Gandhi was being pompous or teasing. All this has to be worked through in order to make sense of identities and events. Nor does Erikson shield himself from such necessary scrutiny. For he accepts that the psychohistorian must include in his analysis 'the inescapable fact that his interpretation is subject to the *mood of his own life,* and heir to a given *lineage of conceptualization'.*[39] How far is it possible to conceptualize Gandhi using an approach developed in the context of a very different culture? And what is the influence of Erikson's own needs? He admits being attracted to his subject-matter not only because he wanted 'to confront the spiritual truth' that Gandhi had formulated and demonstrated in his life with the psychological truth which he himself has learned and practised, but also because 'it was time for me to write about the responsibilities of middle age'.[40]

His approach is coolly clinical as he pieces together evidence into a coherent and plausible pattern. But it is also intense and personal. He tries to create in his own mind – and thus in the reader's – the sound of Gandhi's voice, what he looked like, how he moved. He tries to capture his 'presence' and to get at the 'underlying emotional actuality'.

A letter to Gandhi

Half-way through the book, stung by a remark of Gandhi's addressed to a future reviewer who might seek to analyse his 'pretensions', Erikson breaks off and writes his subject a letter.[41] The effect is startling, rather as if we suddenly encountered them together as patient and therapist. Had Gandhi been alive, one feels he might have been stimulated to look a little differently at himself. At least he would have found it interesting. While Erikson acknowledges his 'abiding and affectionate respect', he confesses to him that

> ... a few times in your work (and often in the literature inspired by you) I have come across passages which almost brought *me* to the point where I felt unable to continue writing *this* book because I seemed to sense the presence of a kind of untruth in the very protestation of truth; of something unclean when all the words spelled out an unreal purity; and above all, of displaced violence where nonviolence was the professed issue.[42]

He goes on to gently chide Gandhi for his pomposity and, in particular, for the underlying tyranny which his moralistic concern for others sometimes seemed to conceal. Erikson perceives a 'certain false pedagogic tone pervading the very kind of apologetic statement which you are apt to use in order to explain, for example, your attempts to impose literacy on your child bride: "But I was a cruelly kind husband. I regarded myself as her teacher and so harassed her out of my blind love for her"'.[43] Admittedly Gandhi had married and become a father while he was himself hardly more than a child. But both his wife and his children suffered a good deal from his 'truly dictatorial combination of maternalism and paternalism' and his inclination to treat those closest to him as 'possessions and whipping posts'. There was little mutuality in his sexual relations with his wife. Initially they took the form of an intense but often guilty indulgence. Later, fearing the detrimental effect of sexual feelings on his spiritual power, he chose celibacy, with little if any reference to her. In the autobiography, he records how he once blamed an illness on his wife's desire to give him food. Elsewhere, he expressed his concern that she may have to appear in court – but only lest her performance should let him down.

The primary example which Erikson cites of Gandhi's despotism concerns an incident at the Ashram – the community he had set up. Gandhi himself tells how, because a youth had 'made fun' of two young girls in the group while they bathed at the spring, he had persuaded the women to cut off their hair. While Erikson takes into account in all such episodes traditional customs and the problem of translation, he also casts a sensitive yet probing eye for possible pretensions and even sexual motivations. He advised Gandhi that 'nonviolence, inward and outward, can become a true force only where ethics replaces moralism'.[44]

Biography as personal construction

By such direct involvement with his subject, Erikson points up the need for the biographer, like the therapist, to be alert to the possibility of *counter-transference* – his own unconscious, emotional projection onto the person he is writing about. Even the very choice of the person to write about may have its roots in early identifications or be a way of indulging suppressed aspects of the writer's own identity – his 'murdered selves'. Such emotional involvement is highlighted by what Erikson calls *cross-transference*. So, because of his sense of a special relationship with Gandhi, he admits to feeling annoyance when other biographers presented his subject in a different way.

Erikson wonders about the possibility of transference in his relations with others involved in Gandhi's story. During his time in India he had stayed with Ambalal, the mill owner who had been Gandhi's benefactor as well as principal opponent in the strike. He speculates on the possibility of unconscious child-parent feelings being projected into the guest-host relationship. He suspects a special vulnerability for himself here because he had never known his own natural father. Although Erikson implies but does not articulate this, we may also wonder whether he chose to focus on the strike event at Ahmedabad (which other commentators and Gandhi himself seem to place less emphasis on) because he happened to be staying in the mill owner's house in the town where it took place.

The significance of all this is that it demonstrates Erikson's attempt to confront the inevitable fact that *any* biography inevitably rests on *construction,* both on the part of the biographer or historian, and of the witnesses who provide the source material. Rather than assuming some spurious objectivity, it is better to consider reflexively, as a good analyst does, the possible effects of this. The result is not just more meaningful psychobiography but a heightening of our awareness of the intrinsic relativity of understanding itself.

Gandhi's life and character

Erikson's book on Gandhi is complex, detailed and discursive. Through the course of over 400 pages he follows Gandhi's progress through his early childhood in the 1870s, marriage at thirteen, his 'experiments with temptation', student days in England, twenty years spent as a barrister and later champion of oppressed Indians in South Africa, his return to India for good and the first dramatic phase of his mature life in his motherland.

Erikson traces the evolution and origins of Gandhi's *identity*: first identifications and conflict resolutions in childhood and family life, his exploration of possible identities during the moratorium of his years in England training to become a barrister, repudiation of the image which the whites of South Africa attempted to thrust upon him and, above all, the strength which he drew from the heritage of his own culture. But in contrast with his treatment of Luther, Erikson's use here of psychoanalytic concepts, both Freudian and his own, is much more restrained. A negative view might attribute this to the greater constraint which the range of available evidence imposed on his scope to shape and reconstruct in line with his theory. More charitably, we may see in it an acknowledgement of the significance of cultural differences. In acknowledgement of this, he does make some attempt to draw on the Hindu conception of the life cycle in his analysis of Gandhi's life. This views a person's current existence as but one phase in a recurring cycle of lives. The foundations for personhood are therefore laid before birth (or rather, in Hindu terms, rebirth). Within the life span, Erikson detects three broad stages: *Antevasin* or Apprenticeship where life skills appropriate to one's caste are developed; *Grhastha* or Householdership which involves full participation in life – in family relations, maintenance of society and sensual enjoyment; and, finally, *Vanaprastha,* the gradual separation from the ties of the world leading to *Moksha* or renunciation. Erikson also brings to bear other Hindu conceptions such as *dharma,* 'a sense of life task determined by previous lives as well as by acquisition and choice'.[45] Thus, Gandhi and Ambalal were able to confront each other without rancour in the strike because they recognized their respective *dharmas* – as mill owner to make money, as priest-politician to fast and strive for the welfare of the oppressed.

Erikson's strength lies precisely in his refusal to be sucked into dogmatic and simplistic reductionism. He has the courage and skill to confront his human material in all its complexity and with due regard for its origins and the problems involved in making sense of it. He is firmly opposed to the fallacy of what he calls '*originology*' – 'the habitual effort to find "causes" of a man's whole development in his childhood conflicts'.[46] He talks of the 'genetic' approach of psychoanalysis as the 'curse' which too often 'leads us to reconstruct a child's development as if it were nothing but the product of his parents' virtues or vices'.[47] He certainly considers 'any attempt to reduce a leader of Gandhi's stature to earlier as well as bigger and better childhood traumata both wrong in method and evil in influence'.[48] In his view Gandhi's achievement

> ... is not a mere matter of projecting the conflicts of his childhood on a widening world of concerns – a crank, a fanatic, and a psychotic could manage that – but one of a minute and concrete interplay, of a craftsmanlike series of 'experiments' with historical actuality in its political and economic aspects.[49]

His awareness of the limitations of investigations extends to a kind of ambivalence about the desirability of 'capture by understanding' even if it should prove possible: 'It is true that the psychoanalytic method rarely contributes much to the explanation of the excellence of a man's performance – which may be just as well, for it permits the factor of giftedness and grace to escape classification and prescription ...'[50]

The pattern which emerges from accounts of Gandhi's childhood years is of truthfulness to himself and others and what seems from the viewpoint of Western culture an almost sycophantic obedience and veneration of his elders. Warmth and religious feeling were the fruits of his young mother's care but for him, the youngest son, the powerful emotional bond was with his much older father.

Erikson speculates on the especial power of Oedipal conflict in boys with outstanding talent. Their conscience, he suggests, develops early and 'they sense in themselves ... some kind of originality that serves to point beyond a mere competition with the personal father's accomplishments'.[51] The intensity of chagrin which Gandhi reported experiencing because he left his father just before the moment when he died in order to make love with his wife, Erikson interprets as a reflection of his underlying feelings of guilt. He traces the Oedipus theme too in Gandhi's particular preferences among mythical tales. (One of these was the story of Phraled. His demon father had been destroyed by God, after he had forced his son to embrace a red-hot pillar of metal because he had refused to acknowledge the greatness of his power!) With some impressive analytic detective work, Erikson even finds a father-son theme reflected in the imagery of Gandhi's political pamphlets. Perhaps there was something of filial obedience, he also suspects, in his curiously unconditional offer to the Viceroy to help recruit for the

British forces in the First World War. A related theme – the sense of being the favoured and most able child – seemed echoed too in Gandhi's continued refrain that he is the *'only one'* who can take effectively whatever action is required.

What really comes across is the complexity and seeming contradictions in Gandhi's character. He was a man whose very humility seemed to spring from a will to power. From being a dandified barrister who could take snobbish delight in travelling first class, he came to practise a militant poverty and be prepared to do for others the meanest of tasks. A delight in teasing and making fun co-existed with a moralism which could lead him to forbid his followers to gossip, sleep too much or to drink tea. He refused to take milk to avoid inflicting pain upon a cow and yet could treat his sons with harsh rejection. The militant Indian who was to be instrumental in weakening colonial rule was also an English gentleman who served the Empire in the Boer War. Erikson's notion of polarities has a field day. For all Gandhi's single-minded simplicity, he can at different times sound like both a socialist and a conservative, a pacificist and a militarist, a stickler for and a breaker of tradition, a nationalist and one who aspires to dissolve such a narrow category for a greater humanity.

Perhaps, though, such seeming inconsistency, as well as his pomposity, sprang from his most enduring characteristic – his candour. All his life he strove after absolute honesty with himself and others. On a conscious level at least, he made no attempt to present himself in a positive or consistent light. Erikson puts it well:

> Here was a man who both lived and wondered aloud, and with equal intensity and depth, about a multiformity of inclinations which other men hide and bury in strenuous consistency. At the end, great confusion can be a mark of greatness, too, especially if it results from the inescapable conflicts of existence.[52]

Gandhi's originality rested on this ruthless honesty and his capacity to listen and act on his 'voice within'. There was a quality of 'mighty drivenness' about him and in his use of the vow as 'a spiritual navel cord'. His intense and flexible energy allowed him to roam India taking little sleep or food. His Christ-like compassion enabled him to turn the other cheek even to the extent of warmly embracing those who before had beaten him up. While being able to delight in life, he was deeply aware too of the nothingness which bounds it. All this combined in a person who Erikson, for want of a better word, calls a *religious actualist* – one who is able to realize his spiritual awareness in the way he lives his life.

Psychosocial analysis

As in his other studies, Erikson does not, of course, neglect the psycho-social nature of his subject-matter. Events and actions take their significance from the meanings they have within the culture in which they occur. Many of Gandhi's characteristics which draw attention in Western eyes – his concern with temptation and ambivalence towards sexuality, for example – can pass unremarked among his compatriots. The quality of androgyny which he radiated and his fatalistic fortitude in the face of suffering also reflect themes which run through Indian history. Indian culture matches Gandhi in its complexity, and its identity eludes easy characterization. On the basis of his experiences in India and extensive reading, Erikson tentatively postulates certain dynamic polarities. On one hand, for example, there is freedom of sexual expression, on the other compulsive order. Meditative passivity is coupled with pragmatism. There is 'an utterly ahistorical sense of living' alongside 'inventories of assembled facts'. One particularly central polarity, which he ascribes to the experience of crowded and extended family life, is that 'between fusion-in-the-mass and utter solitude'.

But Erikson does not take this kind of analysis very far. He is aware of a fundamental problem in approaching India from a Western point of view. Understanding another society requires an appreciation of the world-view in which it is immersed. It is for this reason he endeavoured to draw on and explore Hindu conceptions of life, virtue and humankind. But he acknowledges the problems this involves:

> Such 'principles' as *dharma, Artha* ... and *Moksha*[53] cannot be compared with Western principles in the sense that they provide categorical permissions or prohibitions. Rather, they are forms of *immersion* in different *orders* of *self-abandonment*.[54]

Given the difficulty of translating the concepts of one world-view into another in which there may be no equivalents, Erikson, I think, does a remarkable job in conveying the quality of Indian experience. But he warns that, while such a backcloth is an essential basis for understanding his subject, Gandhi's achievement was to take traditional roles and attitudes and mould them into new and creative forms. While he was rooted in his culture, at the same time he transcended it.

Moral lessons

In his study of Gandhi and his impact, Erikson sought not just to analyse but to learn. The book contains a moral message, one which he made explicit when invited by the students of Cape Town University to lecture to them in 1968.[55] One of the reasons he chose Gandhi as a subject was because he saw the relevance of his example in the political task of countering apartheid, which Erikson considers to be a form of 'pseudo-speciation'. This, as you may remember from the last chapter, is the dangerous inclination of particular human groups to regard themselves and their culture as being the fundamental human form, maintaining this belief by cultural self-idealization and moral and political propaganda. In extreme form, when

> ... we have learned to reduce 'the other' – *any* living human being in the wrong place, the wrong category, or the wrong uniform – to a dirty speck in our moral vision, and potentially a mere target in the sight of our (or our soldiery's) gun, we are on the way to violating man's essence, if not his very life.[56]

The alternative which Gandhi both conceived *and* demonstrated is *Satyagraha*. This word is a Sanskrit combination which he coined, meaning literally 'truth' and 'force'. Its truth aspect lies in its attempt to mobilize honesty in both adversaries in a dispute. Its force lies in its militant assertion of a common humanity. While it proscribes all violence or damage to property, there is also force in the courage and commitment it requires. It is a stance taken up not for want of any alternative but from active choice. It seeks to foster a sense of mutual respect. 'That action alone is just which does not harm either party to a dispute', Gandhi wrote in one of his leaflets to the Ahmedabad strikers. It involves not forcing opponents into an act of submission but of giving them the courage for voluntary change.

> The resister must be consistently *willing* to *persuade* and to enlighten, even as he remains ready *to be persuaded* and enlightened. He will, then, not insist on obsolete precedent or rigid principle, but will be

guided by what under changing conditions will continue or come to feel true to him and his comrades ...[57]

In more recent times, Nelson Mandela who, after his release and becoming President of South Africa, had the wisdom to make peace with some of his old enemies, exemplifies such an approach. Erikson sees in *Satyagraha* hope for humanity, a potential next step in human psychosocial evolution. There are limitations though to its use. Even Gandhi recognized it could only work with an opponent, like the British, who could be stimulated or shamed into a mutually agreeable resolution. Erikson though was optimistic about its potential. In an untypical digression where he draws on Lorenz's ideas about the ritualization of aggression in animals, he suggests the possibility of an 'instinctual' basis for 'pacific' as well as 'pseudospecific' behaviours in humankind. Nevertheless, he realizes that to make *Satyagraha* a widespread social reality will require conscious effort to imbue 'essential daily experiences with a *Satyagraha*-of-every-day-life'.[58] A basic necessity here is to replace *moralism* (blind obedience to dogmatic principles) with *ethics* ('insightful assent to human values'). Combining the insights of Freud with those of Gandhi, he argued that we must also avoid doing violence to our inner, instinctual experience: 'man can find what peace there is in this existence only in those moments when his sensual, logical, and ethical faculties balance each other'.[59]

Gandhi's Truth was awarded the Pulitzer Prize and a National Book Award and translated into several languages. Reviews however were again ambivalent. Psychoanalysts criticized Erikson for making too much of the influence of culture, Indian scholars for taking it insufficiently into account. Its impact on intellectuals and the public did not begin to approach that of his first book *Childhood and Society*.

Given the complexity of his offerings and their refusal to sit neatly within clear disciplinary boundaries, what then does the work of Erikson offer us overall? It is to this question that we now turn in the final chapter of this book.

7 The Nature of Erikson's Contribution

Erikson's death in 1994 was marked by fulsome accolades on the importance of his work. Robert Wallerstein, Chair of Psychiatry at the University of California, San Francisco described his contributions as 'monumental' and went to assert that 'after Freud, no single psychoanalyst has had a more profound impact on our twentieth century culture and world than he'.[1] While not all psychoanalysts would necessarily agree with this, many people did. Even US President Bill Clinton joined in the praise.

> Throughout his long career, countless people turned to Erik's intelligence and insight to explain what humans could not understand about themselves. His pioneering contributions to psychoanalysis changed the ways in which we see our lives and challenged us to reexamine our relationships to the world around us. His work reflects a remarkable breadth of scholarship. More than that, it reveals an extraordinary level of empathy and compassion. He will be sorely missed.[2]

During his career in the USA Erikson went from academic admiration and being lauded as a cultural hero (signified by him being featured on the cover of the New York Times Magazine in 1970) to subsequently being subjected to wide-ranging criticisms. Some orthodox psychoanalysts questioned the emphasis he placed on social influences, leftwingers expressed concern at what they considered to be conservatism and feminists deplored what they saw as a traditional attitude to women. Not only was the quality of his work questioned but, as we shall see, his honesty in his writings about himself. So looking back over the chapters of this book, how can we summarize Erikson's contribution? How should his work be regarded? In what ways does he enlighten us about the nature of the human condition and how we may understand it?

Erikson's work is best regarded as a lineal descendant of Freudian theory. He did not attempt a fundamental restatement of psychoanalytic propositions but his contribution was rather to enrich, clarify and extend it by introducing new significant considerations. Thus, he took far more into account the importance of cultural and historical contexts and was able to illustrate vividly the nature of their influence on individual identity. He is among those contemporary analysts who have deepened our understanding of the functioning of the *ego*. His particular contribution here has been to provide a useful conceptualization of its growth through life; also to illuminate the concept of identity and the processes involved in its development. He has shown how this can be used as a tool for the analysis of both cultures and individuals. In these ways, Erikson was able to achieve a truly *integrative* analysis, taking into account not only early development but social contexts and the course and consequences of psychological development into adolescence and adult life. Erikson's own studies, both clinical and historical, also serve *par excellence* to illustrate what I have argued elsewhere[3] is the most important potential of psychoanalysis, its *hermeneutic* function – its capacity to elicit meaning and offer insights into many aspects of individual and cultural life.

Clinical method

Erikson was renowned for his clinical insights and therapeutic work. Before going on to examine the contribution made by his theoretical and research studies, it is worth looking a little more closely at his clinical approach. This is a less explicit and influential aspect of his work, but he lectured and published papers on it (see especially *Insight and Responsibility*, 1964).[4] As we have seen, a good idea of his clinical style can be gleaned from the many case illustrations he provides. They convey a vivid sense of seeing psychoanalysis in operation.

In many respects, his method is quite orthodox. Where appropriate, he uses standard techniques like dream analysis, free association and working through transference. He works on the basis of the normal psychoanalytic assumptions of unconscious motivation and the significance of early development. He endeavours to trace the shadow which infantile anxieties may cast on adult functioning, to trace the way in which 'the past ... is built into the present ... to help free the present for its future tasks'.[5] But there is also a strongly existential aspect; hinted at perhaps by his use of the word 'client' as well as 'patient'. He is concerned with the way his clients feel, think and make sense of the world. The quality of his empathic sensitivity to this comes across in his alertness to what his youngest clients must feel when they are brought to see him.

> The child has not chosen to come. He often does not feel sick at all in the sense that he has a symptom which he wishes to get rid of. On the contrary, all he knows is that certain things and, most of all, certain people make him feel uncomfortable and he wishes that we would do something about these things and people – not about him. Often he feels that something is wrong with his parents, and mostly he is right. But he has no words for this and, even if he did have, he has no reason to trust us with such weighty information. On the other hand, he does not know what the parents have told us about him – while God only knows what they have told the child about us. For the parents, helpful as they may wish to be and necessary as they are as initial informants, cannot be trusted in these matters: the initial history given is often distorted by the wish to justify (or secretly punish) themselves or to punish (and unconsciously justify) somebody else, perhaps the grandparents who 'told you so'.[6]

In contrast to the orthodox Freudian emphasis on the neutrality of the analyst, Erikson is very active in his therapeutic approach – where children are concerned at least. He involves himself personally, talking and playing with them, even visiting them at home, becoming not just an interpreter but a medium through which they can work through what conflicts they feel.

For Erikson, as for Freud, there is a reciprocal relationship between research and therapy. If clients help provide the data on which his theories depend, this understanding in turn influences his clinical work. Thus Erikson's interest extends to his clients' social contexts, the settings in which they lead their lives. The particular stage of development they have reached may provide useful clues to the underlying nature of problems which beset them. But at the heart of the psychotherapeutic encounter is the subjective experience of both therapist and client and their capacity to share this with each other.

> There is a core of disciplined subjectivity in clinical work and this both on the side of the therapist and of the patient – which it is neither desirable nor possible to replace altogether with seemingly

more objective methods which originate, as it were, in the machine-tooling of other kinds of work. How the two subjectivities join in the kind of disciplined understanding and shared insight which we think are operative in a cure – that is the question.[7]

Although Erikson is committed to sharing interpretations and insights, he is chary about thrusting meanings on his clients, particularly when these may be premature.

> The clinician … has no right to test his reconstructions until his trial formulations have combined into a comprehensive interpretation which feels right to him, and which promises, when appropriately verbalized, to feel right to the patient.[8]

While he admits that it is not easy to ascertain therapeutic success, he sees the proof lying 'in the way in which the communication between therapist and patient "keeps moving" leading to new and surprising insights and to the patient's greater assumption of responsibility for himself'.[9] What comes across is the flexible and undogmatic nature of Erikson's approach and his recognition of the therapist's need to take into account his own emotional input and influence on the proceedings.

Theoretical and research studies

Erikson the integrationist – and its perils

As in his clinical work, his theoretical and research studies were unique in their approach. Erikson was above all an *integrationist* as evidenced by his triple book-keeping approach. He was concerned to understand human behaviour and experience in its totality. If this meant crossing disciplinary boundaries then so be it. His primary roots may have been in psychoanalysis but he also drew on other disciplines – including anthropology, history, psychology, in none of which he had been trained.

An integrative approach is almost invariably a hard road even though it is a very necessary one to follow if full understanding is to be achieved. Academics, like other people, want to belong – to have a specific identity. They also like to know what each other's identifications are and thus where they are coming from. By seeking rich mergers with the knowledge and concepts provided by other fields like anthropology and history, Erikson did for psychoanalysis what it badly needed – to take it out of its insularity. But from his early days in Vienna he was always regarded with a degree of suspicion for his unorthodoxy. Although Erikson tried to avoid controversy and clearly wanted to stay within the fold, eventually Anna Freud and many figures in the psychoanalytic establishment became highly uncomfortable about the intellectual distance he had travelled from them. They criticized him precisely for that for which he was admired by others – his emphasis on the importance of cultural influence. Fortunately by that time, however, he had established his own voice and following in the USA.

If we trace the development of Erikson's life and ideas, we can see the influence of those he encountered reflected in his work. His roots in psychoanalysis were laid down in Vienna with his contacts and training in the very heart of the psychoanalytic establishment. We also see his interest in ego psychology stimulated by his mentors Heinz Hartmann, Paul Federn and by Anna Freud. Anna's interest was in working with children and the particular speciality of another influential figure for Erikson at this time – August Aichhorn, was working with adolescents. And, of course, both child analysis and an interest in adolescence are further themes we see reflected in Erikson's own work.

Once in the USA Erikson not only made much of his contacts but was brought into contact with a range of new ideas. His research work on children with psychologists at Yale and Berkeley yielded material to use in his writings. His trips with Scudder Mekeel and Alfred Kroeber as well as his friendship with Margaret Mead gave him understanding of anthropological observations and insights which he was to make good use of in his studies of Indian tribes. Erikson also relied heavily on his creative and intellectual friends – such as David Rapoport, David Riesman, and later his son Kai for comments and inputs into his own writing and thinking.

This detailing of influences on Erikson's thinking is not meant to imply that his work is derivative. Like many great theorists (Darwin and Freud for example), he stood on the shoulders of others, but made their ideas his own. Like Freud, his great achievement was integrating them into his own coherent vision.

If Erikson drew on the work of others, he was perhaps sometimes slow to acknowledge it. The relation of his work to that of Erich Fromm bears some comment. There were many similarities between the two men. Of similar age (Fromm being two years the senior), both were analysts and emigrés from Germany to the USA. Both were interested in society and its impact on individual identity and took into account existential aspects of being. However there were significant differences. Fromm had received more formal training outside psychoanalysis including a doctorate in sociology from the University of Heidelberg as well as being a research associate at the renowned Frankfurt Institute for Social Research. Fromm was a Marxist and his interest in the impact the alienation of modern society has on identity had been expressed in his 1941 book *Fear of Freedom*. Erikson had certainly read this.[10] He had also with his wife Joan visited Fromm in Mexico though from all accounts there was little discussion of ideas. It seems likely that Fromm's thinking must have had some influence on his own and yet he makes no explicit reference to this. (However it is true that Fromm reciprocated by largely ignoring Erikson's work.)[11]

One reason for Erikson's failure to attribute acknowledgement to Fromm may well have been his concern at not being seen to side with revisionists unacceptable to the psychoanalytic establishment.[12] But in addition, like Fromm, Erikson was an individualist, not willing to follow dogma and concerned with forging his own creative path. For such reasons, Erikson's relations with his co-researchers at Yale and Berkeley were also not always easy. He did not fit comfortably into a research team. What Erikson offered was a unique creative synthesis. He provided some core concepts – such as the life cycle, but by and large it is Erikson's discursive analyses of individuals and societies that make his work so fascinating and stimulating to our thinking about what it is to be human. And these are not easy to reproduce. Nor are they an easy act for followers to pick up on. He leaves behind no specific legacy – no school in his name.

Even ideas which he initiated and were later to become influential were often not attributed to him. For example, his *psychosocial approach* bears resemblance to contemporary versions of *social constructionism*, particularly in more recent attempts to forge links between social analysis and psychoanalysis. Yet he is rarely if ever acknowledged by social constructionists as a predecessor – perhaps because they find unpalatable the emphasis he still retains on individuality rather than the person as wholly constructed by culture. His failure to be acknowledged as an antecedent by social constructionists could also be due to the feminist critiques that were levelled against his research studies claiming morphologically-based differences in the play of boys and girls. His interpretations here were seen, I think unfairly, as representing projections of stereotypical gender differences. (Ironically perhaps, as we have seen, he was conversely criticized by his student Carol Gilligan for assuming that male and female life cycles follow a similar course, rather than the different patterns that she considered to characterize women's lives.)

It is never easy to be an integrationist. But it meant that, although Erikson may have been an intellectual precursor of social constructionism and even anticipated postmodernism, he was never tempted into the excesses of relativism associated with the latter perspective. His triple book-keeping approach kept his analyses firmly grounded in embodied and experiential realities even while he acknowledged the pervasiveness of social influence.

Erikson's legacy has fared little better in the empirical arena. There have been some attempts to test out aspects of his life cycle conception. James Marcia, for example, has used semi-structured interviews to explore how identity develops through young adulthood.[13] Marcia allocates his interviewees to different statuses depending on the amount of identity commitment and exploration they engage in. However, by and large, as Erikson himself would have acknowledged, his ideas are too subtle and elusive to be pinned down in the measurement and categories of empirical work.

Limitations of Erikson's analyses

Even taken on its own terms, however, there are a number of criticisms which can be levelled at Erikson's theoretical work, many of which have already been noted in the preceding chapters. Minor ones include the sometimes considerable similarities in the content of his books – or even straight repetitions; though he expresses the hope that these are 'forgivable as family likenesses'. The full-blown quality of his style and what sometimes seems like a preciosity in his play on words (e.g., his distinctions between 'ritualization' and 'ritualism, 'relativity' and 'relativism', etc.) can be an irritant to some readers too. More serious is the possibility of cultural bias. Although he clearly recognizes that his conceptualizations of identity and the life cycle are centred in contemporary Western life, he is still tempted to use them (as in the case with Luther, for example) when they may not be applicable in the same way. As we have noted, his conceptualization of women has also been criticized. On those occasions where his analysis does shift from its tendency to treat masculine experience as the universal human condition, it can be inclined to sound patronizing.

While there is no doubt about the vigour of Erikson's work, questions can be raised about its rigour. However sensible his ideas may sound, he is sometimes prone to dogmatic pronouncements entirely unsupported by argument or evidence. As but one example, take this statement on schizophrenia:

> No matter what conditions may have caused a psychotic break, the bizarreness and withdrawal in the behaviour of many very sick individuals hides an attempt to recover social mutuality by a testing of the borderlines between senses and physical reality, between words and social meanings.[14]

There is a quality of imprecision about some of his writings which allows readers considerable latitude to take from it what they will. As he admitted disarmingly in the BBC radio interview I did with him:

> Without trying to, or wanting to, I just happen to have the kind of artistic temperament that in a book leads me to express my experience in my own way. That often is somewhat seductive for many readers. I've read it over and over again that people felt something, found it very good and found it very convincing and afterwards they didn't quite know what I had said. So my readers have to be warned there.[15]

And a little later,

> I think one could be more precise than I am, or than I am able to be. I very much feel that scientific training and logic would have helped a lot.[16]

Given such charming frankness, it would seem churlish to pursue the point. It will suffice to bring to mind a few examples already encountered. Very occasionally, there is the inconsistent way in which a term may be employed to refer to different things, as in the case of 'negative identity'. Or, to take another example, there is the use, without comment, of 'self-absorption' as a possible counterpart to *both* 'intimacy' and 'generativity'. It is not that any of these necessarily matter much in themselves but they can convey some sense of confusion.

Of more major concern to any sceptical academic who values rigour is Erikson's tendency to go well beyond the information given. We find this in some of the major themes in his analysis of Luther and also in small comments made in passing. On what basis, one wonders, was Erikson justified in commenting about a patient as he does, when he was not even present at the scene, that 'there is no doubt that there was triumph as well as fear in the eyes of that little girl'.[17] Imaginative reconstruction this may be but it does raise legitimate doubts about what means there are for assessing the validity of his complex configurations. The rigorous critic is hardly likely to be convinced by criteria like the one Erikson suggested in our radio discussion – a readiness in the consciousness of people 'so that when they hear it they immediately feel "yes this is me and this my problem"'.[18]

Curiously, it does not take a great deal of effort to see in some of these supposed weaknesses the basis of a virtue. With his commonsensical and non-doctrinaire approach, Erikson resists the temptation to formulate neat laws and propositions precisely to avoid the attendant risks of over-simplification and reification. If he declines to provide pat definitions of complex, intangible concepts like identity, it is because he believes that it is better to delineate by displaying such concepts in use rather than risk the distortion and the fossilization that can ensue from encapsulation in neat phrases.

I do not think the problem of validity arises either out of Erikson's neglect or his deficiency. Aware of the dangers of aggrandizing a concept 'to become the universe ... the prime reality', he is usually careful to be tentative in his interpretations. He knows the difficulties of evaluating a pattern put together from fragmentary clues yielded by observations and inference. The problem of validity (in the sense of assessing whether an interpretation is correct or not) arises rather because it may not be an *appropriate* criterion to apply to the kind of task in which he is engaged. For there is no straightforward, formal way of testing whether interpretations of this kind are right or wrong. How could you evaluate precisely, for example, inferences as to the meaning and intention underlying a young child's action? You can only ask: is the pattern consistent? Does it help to make sense of the total pattern of his behaviour? Does it illuminate your observations and give to a sequence of events a meaning more profound than that which existed before? Whatever the interpretation, there is no way of knowing for sure whether, with further information or exploration, it will continue to hold up. Interpretation is inevitably provisional.

Such intractable problems arise because psychoanalysis involves the study of *meaning*. The most effective way we have of conveying the complex meanings of mental life is through the medium of *language* (though not necessarily by means of the face value of what is said. As Erikson has put it, some 'things are hard to say, and wording is not too important. What counts is their spirit...'). Indeed, it could be argued that skill in using language is an important element in the creation of meaning itself. It is no coincidence that both Freud and Erikson are noted for their literary styles. (Erikson comments that Freud's writings seem 'to reflect the very creativity of the unconscious'.) Words are the essential tools of their trade.

A core feature of language is an inherent ambiguity. In part this arises from its structural nature which makes meaning dependent on context. This operates at several levels and involves both linguistic and social settings. Thus whether 'o' is a letter or a number is only made clear by what precedes or follows it. Whether 'sail' is a noun or verb is only apparent when we see the sentence in which it is used. Knowing whether 'I am sorry' is sarcastic or genuine depends on hearing the conversation of which it is a part. And the meaning of that conversation itself will be significantly different if it is with a friend rather than part of a play. This contextual basis of language is its strength. It makes possible the subtlety, variety and novelty of which it is capable. But it is not surprising therefore if the exploration of underlying meanings – the essential task of the analyst – is also coloured by a similar quality of ambiguity and lack of precision. This is in keeping with the essential nature of its subject matter. It is now also perhaps apparent why both Erikson's writings, as well as this account of them, are in somewhat discursive style. A set of simply packaged propositions could not put across effectively the meanings they would be required to convey.

In dealing with meaning we do not just have to consider its inherent ambiguity but, as with any other kind of understanding, the principle of *relativity* as well. In other words, it is important to recognize that it can *only* be grasped by some form of interpretation or reconstruction. Meaning exists only from the perspective of some particular point of view. It is not some neutral or 'objective' abstraction. Any interpretation should therefore include some attempt to take into account the character of its own construction. Habermas[19] has suggested that no discipline is more fitted to this task of reflexive examination than psychoanalysis; and, as we saw in his study of Gandhi, Erikson is only too prepared to subject his interpretations to such scrutiny.[20]

What is it then that Erikson has produced? It is hardly equivalent to the biological and natural sciences with their requirements of precision, repeatable observations and testable hypotheses. There is a quality of art about it. He does offer portraits sketched with clarity and obscurities, with the multiple facets of a Picasso picture. But it also differs from art or its literary equivalent – the novel. For his work is intrinsically concerned with specific actualities. There is a firm commitment to understanding the way things are. There is an immersion in his subject-matter, as well as a capacity for empathy, which brings to mind Einstein's dictum that a great scientist is like 'one who is in love'. Perhaps the best way we can describe his work is as truly *psychosocial science*. Boldly crossing the boundaries of disciplines, Erikson provides a 'conceptual itinerary' to help us make sense of the lives of ourselves and others. He presents us with analyses of the configurations of meaning in an action, a person or a culture, without sacrificing subtlety and the complexity of the underlying integration which each represents. Such analyses are not easy either to carry out or assimilate. They require a high level of individual skill and tolerance of ambiguity, the capacity to hold in mind a series of configurations as possible working hypotheses and to adopt a critical yet flexible attitude to determine which has the greater consistency and best fits the available clues. But it is precisely Erikson's attempt to struggle with the complexity of his subject-matter rather than choose methods because they are neater and easier to execute, that constitutes his achievement. He recognizes that

> When it comes to central aspects of man's existence, we can only conceptualize at a given time what is relevant to us for personal, for conceptual, and for historical reasons. And even as we do so, the data and the conclusions change before our eyes. Especially at a time when our conceptualizations and interpretations become part of a historically self-conscious scene, and when insight and conduct influence each other with an immediacy that hardly leaves a pause for any new 'tradition' to form – in such a time all thinking about man becomes an experiment in living. The newness of man's self-awareness and of his attention to his awareness has, at first, led to a scientific mythology of the mind or to a mythological use of scientific terms and methods, as if social science could and would repeat in a short time, and in view of immediate practical goals, the whole long progress of natural science from nature philosophy to pure and applied science. But man, the subject of psychosocial science, will not hold still enough to be divided into categories both measurable and relevant.[21]

One test of the effectiveness of Erikson's concepts in helping us to make sense of personal life is to apply them in thinking about your own self and your own situation. For those readers interested in trying this, I have included a few activities which may be of help in an appendix – *Exercises in Self-Awareness* at the end of this chapter.

Personal construction

Erikson himself was in no doubt that our behaviour and creations are related to our personality and situation. So what kind of person was he? And how did his identity and work emerge out of his life experiences? What are the possible sources, personal as well as intellectual, of Erikson's ideas and approach, and of his particular strengths and weaknesses?

We have already had an overview of Erikson's life in Chapter 2. In keeping with the reflexiveness which one might expect of a good analyst, Erikson himself also provides us with some useful clues. He has written, if not an autobiography, then autobiographical notes in the form of an essay, originally for *Daedalus*, called *'Identity Crisis' in Autobiographic Perspective*.[22] While this has been criticized[23] as rather superficial and serene and implausible as a full account of crisis in his life, if we supplement it by hints elsewhere in his books and personal communications, it does allow us to detect one or two possibly significant themes.

At school, young Erik had a particular interest in history, laying perhaps the foundations for his later concern with historical and geographical contexts of individuals and cultures. His early grounding in classical languages may well have given him an awareness of the significance of and a feel for the subtleties of meaning. Erikson admits to a lack of philosophical and scientific training and it may be this which is partly responsible for his later reluctance to generate formal propositions and hypotheses and grand theories.

Where psychoanalysis was concerned, Freud of course was the most powerful influence. But Erikson followed the spirit rather than the dogmatic letter of his work just as Freud himself would have done, had he found himself in his place. In terms of specific interests and the focus of his work we can trace the influence of the mentors who trained and encouraged him in Vienna. As we noted earlier, Anna Freud specialized in the analysis of children and, like his other teachers, Hartmann and Kris, came to place much stress on ego functioning. The speciality of another supervisor, Aichhorn, had been therapeutic work with delinquent adolescent boys.

There seem to have been two predominant role models in Erikson's life. One was *doctor*, like his stepfather and many of his later associates in Vienna. Erikson in fact attributed Freud's powerful impact on him in part to 'some strong identification with my stepfather, the pediatrician, mixed with a search for my own mythical father'.[24] He certainly emotionally identified with Freud, noting how they had both been close to their Jewish mothers and had both been 27 before leaving their families to set up independent lives. The other role was *artist*, the profession of several friends of his mother whom he had known as a child, and his own initial choice for a career. His abiding interest and skill in art may well have provided the basis for his impressionistic and configurational approach. Erikson himself acknowledges this.

> I came to psychology from art, which may explain, if not justify, the fact that at times the reader will find me painting contexts and backgrounds where he could rather have me point to facts and concepts. I have had to make a virtue out of a constitutional necessity by basing what I have to say on representative description rather than on theoretical argument.[25]

Visual and sensory experience precede the ability to verbalize. Our deepest emotions and motivations are probably experienced most fundamentally as feelings or images rather than in verbal form. Erikson's background in art, therefore, may have considerable relevance to his skill as an analyst, especially in his analysis of children.

> I began to perceive how important visual configurations were, how they actually preceded words and formulations: certainly dreams are visual data, and so is children's play, not to speak of the 'free associations' which often are a series of images, pure and simple – only later put into words.[26]

Erikson sees studying art rather than biological or social science at university as having other kinds of advantage. By leaving him 'equidistant' from biology, psychology and sociology, he feels he is in a better position to achieve some kind of integrated approach. What is sacrificed in detail is made up for in balance.

The sense of being an outsider, of living on boundaries runs through Erikson's life and work. He describes it as his 'stepson theme'. 'Throughout my career I worked in institutional contexts for which I did not have the usual credentials – except, of course, for my psychoanalytic training proper'.[27] It comes out in his forays across disciplinary lines; in his concern with young people who are themselves at the boundary between child and adult. It is reflected in his changing national status from Dane to German to American.

Among the most significant features of Erikson's life must have been his own rootless background – as a child, a wandering youth and an adult immigrant. In the USA, he had to begin work again with patients reared in a different kind of society. Not surprisingly, he was alerted to the importance of culture. His own status as an immigrant in a country consciously concerned to forge a new national identity for its members from so many diverse backgrounds, must also have made him only too aware of the significance of identity.

Yes, if ever an identity crisis was central and long drawn out in somebody's life it was so in mine. Let me tell you some of my marginalities. To begin with I never knew my father. Both my parents were Danish, but they were separated when I was born and my mother first raised me among strangers, in Germany.

Eventually, she married my pediatrician and I grew up in Karlsruhe in Baden. He was Jewish. I was blond and grew tall and the Jewish boys nicknamed me 'the goy'. In school, I became a German superpatriot to live down my Danishness (the Danes wanted to steal Schleswig-Holstein, you remember) and then found that my Jewishness was too much for the patriots, and their anti-Semitism too much for me. In adolescence, I was morbidly sensitive but luckily also gifted enough to become a plausible artist of the wandering type, then in Europe a sort of transitional beatnik. And I did wander, in the Black Forest, the Alps, and in Northern Italy. This made me sturdy physically and balanced in a sensory way: drawing is a good way to become observant. Later psychoanalysis added a certain inner sturdiness; but I often wonder whether this prone and wordy procedure is good for people who have not been ambulatory and generally curious first. Maybe, because of all of this, I recognized in maladjusted children and youths the need to move and not just feel driven and to reflect on it. At any rate, in formulating all that, I found my style and professional identity, which must be one explanation for the impact of *Childhood and Society*. But a condition for my effort was, of course, the fact that the Freudian circle in Vienna were hospitable to an occasional non-physician and provided full training.

Then I met Joan, who was studying European schools of dancing. She is Canadian and the daughter of an Episcopal minister. We married and came to this country. That meant I had to acquire a new language in my thirties, while of all things German certainly the language had become most part of me; but luckily the German 'Humanistische Gymnasium' had also provided me with a good foundation in Latin and Greek.

In the American Psychoanalytic Association I was probably the only member who had not completed any kind of college. But, being a fully trained psychoanalyst, I received only support. Only, when made a training analyst, I could train no one but physicians. In the meantime, Harvard, in 1934, had found a place for me on the Medical School Faculty. You can see, I had to strive doubly to become a reliable professional man, without sacrificing my privilege to roam and to observe.

You rightly ask about the Jewish part of my background as an identity issue: my mother's family was Jewish, but in Denmark baptism and intermarriage are old customs, so one of my ancestors (so she told me) was chief rabbi of Stockholm and another a church historian and pastor in H.C. Anderson's home town.

I have kept my stepfather's name as my middle name out of gratitude (there is a pediatrician in me, too) but also to avoid the semblance of evasion.

But I think that one's sense of identity should not be restricted to what one could not deny if questioned by a bigot of whatever denomination. It should be based on what one can assert as a positive core, an active mutuality, real community. This would force fewer people to become (because they try too hard to become) radical and religious caricatures. It would also force a new standard on communities: do they or do they not provide a positive, a nonneurotic, sense of identity? Jewishness as such has meant little to me, although I would consider some of the Jewish elements in psychoanalysis ancestral in my work. What some genuinely Lutheran elements in Christianity have come to mean to me is indicated in my book on young Luther.

So, it is true, I had to try and make a style out of marginality and a concept out of identity-confusion. But I also have learned from life histories that everything that is new and worth saying (or worth saying in a new way) has a highly personal aspect. The question is only whether it is also generally significant for one's contemporaries. That I must let you judge.[28]

Others did judge – in that they evaluated this autobiographical statement. An ambivalent review by Berman in the New York Times is characterized by a curious mixture of petty carping and fulsome praise. He specifically criticizes the account as being too unreal – as containing no real crises or problems of the kind that dog most people's lives. What particularly upset Erikson about the review, however, was Berman's accusation that he denied his Jewishness and of his 'cosmic chutzpah' in 'inventing himself' by taking the name of Erik Erikson.[29] While it may be true that Erikson's account may skirt round negative aspects of his life, I think the latter charges tells us more about Berman than Erikson. Erikson is particularly concerned about transcending the petty pseudospeciation that identifying with particular cultures, Jewish or otherwise can create. His change of name could equally be regarded as a celebration of that transcendence rather than a denial of his origins.

However, there are certainly aspects of Erikson not revealed or hinted at in this account. Erikson's notions of *paradox and polarity* could be tellingly applied to himself. Here is a man who concerned himself with the care of his child clients, and yet whom his own children found it difficult to be close to. Here also is a man who asserted the value of love and care, and yet consigned his own Down's Syndrome son to an institutional life, publicly concealing his existence, scarcely visiting him, not even attending his funeral. Erikson's fame rested on the new paths he opened up for psycho-analysis, and yet quietly conservative, he did all he could to avoid rejec-tion from the psychoanalytic community for the boldness of his ideas. He is accused of conservatively accepting the *status quo* and yet is the bio-grapher of the great rebels of history Luther and Gandhi. He progressed his career through his social contacts and yet, while at Harvard refused to accept the President's wife into his seminar. While Erikson's writings express his unique voice, they depended on the editorial and research support of others – not just his students but also his wife and son Kai. Here is a man who built his ideas also on the influences of others, and yet was renowned for the originality and pioneering nature of his ideas. We can see that Erikson's own life manifested the complexity and elusiveness of identity about which he writes.

The contemporary relevance of Erikson's ideas

So what value do Erikson's ideas have for us today? Erikson makes clear how we can only be open to the issues which are crucial to our time. Thus, as we have noted, for Freud at the turn of the twentieth century, it was sexuality; for Erikson in the second part of the same century it was identity. It could be argued that, given our increasing globalization and social complexity, the search for identity and an authentic voice is as much a problem for us in the twenty-first century as it was for people in Erikson's time.

I hope that Erikson's ideas and concepts that have been presented in the preceding chapters have resonated in your own experience; that they do not only offer a way of understanding psychological phenomena but have personal relevance as well. So, for example, his conception of the life cycle can stimulate our thinking about our own progression through life and about how ego characteristics such as care and love may have emerged in our own development. Erikson's discussions of identity – and the concepts he introduces such as crisis, moratorium diffusion – may also help us to think about the origins of our own identities and how we might develop these in the future.

Three crucial contributions

Erikson has been presented in this book as representing the essential spirit of psychoanalysis. Without changing the fundamental tenets of Freudian theory, he has succeeded in extending them in a creative and illuminating way. To conclude this evaluation of Erikson's contribution I would like to draw attention to three general aspects of his work which help us to appreciate more clearly what is involved in understanding the human condition and ourselves.

1. Biology and meaning

First is the way he has faced up more directly than his predecessors to the Janus face of human beings – our roots in both biology and symbolic experience. In many respects, this might be regarded as the key issue which confronts those who would make sense of human behaviour and experience. At one level we are biological beings rooted in physical needs and processes, and our behaviours are open to causal analysis of a determinist kind. At the same time, our biological equipment gives us the capacity for symbolic thought and reason and the ability to reflect on ourselves. The open, rule-based processes on which both language and behaviour depend enable us to generate novel sequences of speech and behaviour. Reasons as well as causes become the basis for explanation. It is the interface between these two fundamentally different but related realms of discourse that is the critical issue that psychology needs to address. Erikson, with his emphasis on integration and the functions of the ego, and in his concern with concepts like triple book-keeping and identity, makes a powerful, albeit discursive, assault on this problem.

2. The nature of psychological understanding

Erikson's second general contribution is to make us more aware of the nature of knowledge itself. As we have seen, his concern with *relativity* emphasizes how all theories and understanding of mental life, as well as any evaluations of their worth, are rooted in some personal and cultural background. None can be intrinsically objective, nor is there any fundamental standpoint against which they can be judged. All one can hope to do is to explore interrelationships between and within them and try to be as aware as possible of the origins and character of the particular form of conceptualization being used.

Another interesting epistemological feature, as we have seen, is the use of paradox and polarities which runs throughout his work. There is a temptation at first, when confronted with a statement like 'James' later philosophy became at once a continuation and an abrogation of his father's philosophy', to dismiss the conjunction of opposites as sloppy thinking – as a refusal or inability to be precise about what he means. But it soon becomes apparent that the interplay of polarities is intrinsic to Erikson's way of thinking. It is on this, he considers, that much of mental and cultural life depends. Thus the essential function of the ego is 'to blend opposites without blunting them'.[30] Ego strengths emerge from a sequence of dynamic oppositions. Even 'a nation's identity is derived from the ways in which history has, as it were, counterpointed certain opposite potentialities; the ways in which it lifts this counterpoint to a unique style of civilization, or lets it disintegrate into mere contradiction'.[31]

Erikson is not the first psychoanalyst to emphasize the play of oppositional forces underlying experience. Ambivalence – where someone at the same time may want and not want or both love and hate – is a fundamental feature of the psychoanalytic conception of the human mind. Otto Rank elevated the opposition between the desire to be autonomous and the need to be secure to a central role in personality dynamics. Originating in the act of being born, this polarity may then be echoed throughout life in the many situations where desire for independence and fear of separation conflict. Polarity is also a key theme in the ideas of Carl Jung. The more an aspect of personality is developed in conscious active life, for example, the more he considers its opposite characteristic will be emphasized in the unconscious. Psychological maturity comes with the capacity to express and integrate opposing tendencies in personality.

It is Erikson though who makes the most extensive use of oppositions both in his mode of thinking and writing and in his conceptualization of the phenomena he deals with. He sees paradox, for example, as inherent in religion. He points to Luther's belief in a Christ who is 'unique in all creation and yet lives in each man', and his concern that 'the worst temptation is not to have any', for 'one can be sure that God is most angry when He does not seem angry at all'. We might add that such paradox is evident in other religions too. For the Buddhist the way to master fate is to submit utterly to it.

Paradox and polarity are uncomfortable notions for minds trained in the linear logic of the standard Western world where something which is p cannot at the same time be *not p*. But Erikson reminds us of the need for dialectical thinking in the world of the human psyche. Its essential qualities will elude the grasp of more linear modes of thought.

3. Existential and moral insights

The third general aspect is concerned with the existential and moral implications of his work. It could be argued that Freudian theory has served to undermine our capacity for faith for it helps us to become all too aware of the possibility of an irrational basis on which any belief or ideology may be built.[32] While Erikson recognizes the importance of understanding how the past and the present context impact unconsciously on our lives, he also acknowledges our need for truths to live by, for *beliefs and values to guide our lives*. More than perhaps any other psychoanalyst, he has been concerned with the moral predicaments of human existence, the development and maintenance not just of psychological adjustment but of positive well-being. At the individual level, he has expressed this by exploring the kind of problems and choices we face at different stages of our lives, and articulating the processes on which our sense of personal being depends. At the level of society, he has pointed to the consequences of the way we bring up our children for the sort of society we can expect to have; and the way that unconscious infantile fears can influence political and international relations. He is particularly concerned with the dangers which arise from our tendency to pseudospeciation. In his analysis of Gandhi's *Satyagraha,* he explores possible ways of dealing with this and of finding a way forward to a new positive phase of human psychosocial development.

The moral insights Erikson provides are not prescriptions of a fixed or definitive kind. This for him would have been essentially at odds with the nature of knowledge and the sort of ethics which humanity needs. For prescriptions which are firm and specific can only be a kind of prejudice – 'an outlook characterized by prejudged values and dogmatic divisions; here everything seems to be clearly delineated and compartmentalized, and this by "nature", wherefore it must stay forever the way it always has been'.[33]

The world and humankind are complex and multifaceted. They change as we look at them and open them up to conceptualization from a multiplicity of perspectives. Erikson's way forward is to offer us rather a frame of mind – 'tolerant of differences, cautious and methodical in evaluation, just in judgement, circumspect in action, and – in spite of all this apparent relativism – capable of faith and indignation'.[34] In such ways, he helps us to understand the nature of human needs and the shaping force of human society. He alerts us to their potentials both for good and evil. With the help of his analyses and insights we can become more aware both of the complexities and of the possibilities of human existence.

Appendix: Some Tools for Self-Awareness

The following activities, together with Erikson's concepts and the discussion of them in the text, may help to deepen self-awareness and alert you to possible ways of thinking about yourself and others and the kind of person you might become.

In doing the exercises (particularly those which encourage you to think about different aspects of your life), bear in mind that *any* understanding of mental life is a construction and represents just *one* way of making sense of it. There will never be a definitive hard-and-fast account (at least not one that is valid) which encapsulates what you are and why you are that way.

Exercises 1 and 2 are preliminary, designed to develop your capacity for *inner awareness*. Exercises 3 and 4 are intended to help you to explore where you are in the *life cycle* and how your *relationships* fit in with this. The remaining exercises are focused on different aspects of *identity* and how you experience yourself now. The final two exercises try to help you to begin to open up *new possibilities* – for what you might become and do in the future.

It is best to attempt only one or at most two of these exercises at any one time. You should begin by setting aside an undisturbed period of time for this. But gradually try, as with the concepts and ideas presented in this book, to incorporate them into the pattern of your everyday life. The aim is to become more aware both of how you experience and behave, and also of your potentials for the person you can become.

Opening up awareness

Our heads are full of thoughts, anxieties, wishes, concerns about the past and future. It is not always easy to focus our awareness on what we are experiencing, to introspect upon our feelings. These first two exercises are intended to help you to do this.

1 Getting inside yourself

1. Find a quiet place where you will not be disturbed and lie on the floor with your eyes closed. Breathe slowly and deeply but easily. Try to relax your body as far as you can.
2. Then, focus on your right foot and leg. Tense them hard. Hold this tension for three to four seconds, then relax. Repeat this tensing and relaxing procedure twice. Continue in the same fashion, tensing and relaxing three times in succession the left leg and foot, buttocks and pelvis, pressing the pit of the back to the floor, tensing and relaxing chest and shoulders, right arm and hand, left arm and hand, shoulders and face muscles.
3. Lie still again, breathing slowly and deeply but in a relaxed way. Try consciously to ease any tensions. Once or twice, tense up your whole body, hold it tense for several seconds, then relax back again as before. Try to empty your mind.
4. Then focus your attention on the soles of your feet. Imagine yourself entering your body at that point and slowly wander up the legs and explore each part of the body. Try to become aware of every sensation in the part on which you are concentrating – pressures, tensions, aches, pains, feelings, cold, warmth, expansions, etc. Focus on sensation: don't try to evaluate or think what you should feel. Just experience. Keep your eyes shut, become aware of the different parts of your body and their relationship to each other. (If you feel like moving or stretching at any point, feel free to do so.)
5. This exercise should be repeated over several days. Gradually you should become aware of sensations within you that you normally ignore.

2 Here and now

The aim of this activity is to encourage you to focus as intensively as possible on your immediate flow of awareness – on what you experience *here and now*.

1. Make yourself comfortable and *relax* for a while, breathing slowly, steadily and deeply, but without effort.
2. Let your mind focus on your *sensory experience* – whatever you can see, hear, smell and taste. You might like to focus on each modality in turn, or you may prefer to allow whichever sense dominates your attention at any one time to do so. Try to be aware both of what you are experiencing (e.g., I am aware of a silky patterned blue surface; I am aware of a noise like a car engine revving up in the distance) and also of what the process of being consciously aware of focusing your attention in this way feels like (e.g., does it give you a sense of alertness or aliveness?)
3. After a while, close your eyes and shift your attention to *bodily sensations*. Are you aware, for example, of the sensation of your clothes against your skin and, if you are sitting, the pressure of the seat against your backside? Can you sense any tension? Where? Or does your body feel completely relaxed?
4. Then turn your focus on your *feelings*. What are you feeling at this particular moment? If that feeling leads to a chain of further emotions or even thoughts, let them come, all the time trying to experience fully each emotion as it arises. Some people claim that if you can give yourself up fully to any negative feeling which arises – such as jealousy, guilt or resentment – then it disappears. Giving yourself up to positive feelings, however, intensifies them. Try this out when you can and see if it works for you.
5. Finally, let your mind *go free*, following whatever images or fantasies emerge.

You can also try this exercise with a partner. In this case, express your experience aloud. Your partner's task is to help keep you focused on your 'here and now' experience and to stop you thinking about events or thoughts outside this, or thinking *about* your experience rather than directly experiencing. When your mind starts to wander, he or she should try to bring you back to focusing on what you are aware of.

In everyday living, try to become more aware of impulses within yourself – the way you feel, what you want. Admit them to full awareness (you don't necessarily have to act on them!) Try to focus on what you really feel, not on the way you think you are supposed to feel. Open yourself also to the possibility of 'peak experiences'– those occasional moments of experience when an image, feeling, sight or sound fills you with delight. When and if such moments occur, stop for a while and focus your total awareness on them.

The life cycle and social context

3 Stages of life

1. Go back over Chapter 4 on Erikson's conception of the *eight ages of life*.
2. Can you plot something of your own development through these? *Where do you locate yourself at present?* Remember that, according to Erikson, you would expect to be focally concerned with the issues of more than one stage.
3. Go back through each of the eight stages and jot down notes as far as you can about *your own life pattern* in relation to each stage.
   • What kinds of residue do you feel the *earlier ones* have left in your present self (e.g., questions of trust/mistrust, shame/confidence in yourself, assertiveness, identity).
   • Think through the *future trajectory* of your life. How will you come to terms with the stages yet to come?
4. Think of *people you know* at different stages of life – your children, for example, contemporary friends, older people like your parents. How well does Erikson's analysis fit their concerns and help you to understand them better?

4 Relationships and community

1. Reflect on the particular social contexts in which you live, for example, immediate relationships, your work and the different aspects of the wider society of which you are a part.
2. For each one, ask these questions:
   • What important needs does this fulfil?
   • How far is it appropriate to the stage of development which you have reached?

- Are there any ways in which it fails to fit with what you are and need?
- Are there any ways in which you can change it so that it suits your needs better?

Identity

5 Exploring identity

Reflect on your own identity by trying to apply the concepts discussed in Chapter 5. How do you see your own identity pattern and the way it has developed? Can you detect any key identifications, repudiations, negative identifications, crisis points, or the influence of contexts in which you grew up and now live.

6 Who am I?

1. Ask yourself the question 'Who am I?' at least ten times and write each answer on a separate piece of paper. Try and include in your answers those aspects of yourself which you feel to be most basic and central to you and which express who you really are. Each answer may take any form you feel appropriate – the expression of a feeling, image, role, profession, personality characteristic, age, symbol, etc.
2. Look through your answers and *rank order* them by putting a number on the back from 1 onwards in order of importance.
3. Place them face down in order. Then turn up the least important and concentrate on it for a while. What does it really mean? Ask yourself what you would be and what life would be like if that was not part of you.
4. Go through each answer in turn, from the least to the most important, repeating the same procedure.
5. By the time you reach the last few, you may have become aware of other important aspects of your identity not included in these initial statements.

7 Who are you?

If you can work with a trusted friend (or even two) to help each other explore yourselves, you might try the following technique.

1. One person continuously repeats to the other the question 'Who are you?' in as many different ways as possible (e.g., *who* are you?, who *are* you?, who are *you*?)

2. With each answer, the person responding tries to go deeper and deeper into what he or she is – through roles, physical and personality characteristics to deeper feelings about the self.
3. If after continuing for some time you feel you are not progressing, try varying the questions and probe further the nature of the answers given.

8 Images of self

As we have seen in the discussion of Erikson's work, much of our most potent and emotional awareness comes in the form of images and sensations rather than words. Trying to think of yourself and your identity through images, as opposed to articulating this in words, may throw up some interesting insights.

1. Note down the *metaphors* which you feel best describe what you feel yourself to be (e.g., a reefed ship sailing through rough seas, a bud about to burst into flower, a house falling apart at the seams, etc.). Go through these and analyse their properties. Why do they seem to fit you and your situation?
2. Another more unusual and difficult technique which some people find produces interesting results, is to *imagine entering yourself and travelling deep into your inner layers*. Open yourself to whatever images spontaneously arise. This is best done while relaxed in a quiet and darkened room. You may find yourself encountering scenes from your past or childhood, or images of places and events which somehow seem to personify you. Don't hurry or force the journey. Let the images arise as far as possible of their own accord. Don't analyse them, just experience them.
3. Afterwards, you can recall and examine what you came up with in these two exercises for what they might tell you about yourself and feelings.

9 People you love

1. Think of several specific *people whom you love and/or admire*. Jot down brief notes on the kinds of people they are. How would you describe each one? What is it about them that you particularly like? Is there anything about them that you also find irritating?
2. Do the same with your *parents*. What kind of people are/were they? What are/were their positive and negative aspects? Try to do this in terms of how you see them now and how you saw them when you were growing up.

3. Look back over your notes. Are there *patterns and consistencies?* Do they tell you anything about *your* own self and the ideals you aspire to?

10 Polarities

A bird in my garden comes for food. She pecks at the bread with a constant watchfulness for possible threat. She is poised between the dynamic tension of attraction and flight.

1. Think about the *polarities* which seem to underlie your behaviour and experience. Is there a dynamic tension, for example, between the need to be autonomous and independent and the need for security and deep involvement with others; the need to be adventurous and the need to play it safe?
2. Try to make a list of the most *significant* ones in your self.
3. Consider in each case how you come to terms with it. What patterns of *behaviour and feelings emerge from the interplay* between the polarities?

Creating yourself

11 Creating an action

1. Think of something you would like to do but would not ordinarily do (e.g., going to a museum, taking a taxi instead of a bus, giving a present to someone, speaking to someone you would like to get to know).
2. Imagine yourself doing this.
3. Do it. Be aware that you have chosen to do it and have created an action which otherwise would not have happened.

12 Creating your life

Gradually widen the scope of Exercise 11.

1. Try behaving towards others, for example, in a way that you would like to but would not normally do. You might want just to smile more often, for example. Or to make a conscious effort to do small acts of kindness.
2. Try to help to make things happen which you would like to bring about but would not normally bother, hope or dare to do.

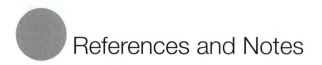

References and Notes

Chapter 1 Introducing Erik H. Erikson (pages 1–5)

1 Elizabeth Mayer (1998) 'Erik H. Erikson on Bodies, Gender, and Development', in R.S. Wallerstein and L. Goldberger (eds) *Ideas and Identities: The Life and Work of Erik Erikson*, Madison, International Universities Press, p.79.
2 Stephen Seligman and Rebecca Shanok (1998) 'Erikson, Our Contemporary: His Anticipation of an Intersubjective Perspective', in Wallerstein and Goldberger, p.327.
3 Paul Roazen (1976) *Erik H. Erikson: The Power and Limits of a Vision*, New York, The Free Press, pp.viii–ix.
4 Laurence Friedman (1998) 'Erik H. Erikson's Critical Themes and Voices: The Task of Synthesis', in Wallerstein and Goldberger, p.353.
5 W.H. Auden (1973) *Forewards and Afterwards*, London, Faber and Faber, p.86.
6 Kit Welchman (2000) *Erik Erikson: His Life, Work and Significance*, Buckingham, Open University Press, p.viii.
7 Francis Gross (1987) *Introducing Erik Erikson: An Invitation to his Thinking*, Lanham, University Press of America, p.3.
8 Erich Fromm is the subject of another book in the Mindshaper series. See Annette Thomson (2008) *Erich Fromm, Explorer of the Human Condition*, Basingstoke, Palgrave Macmillan.
9 Richard Stevens (2008) *Sigmund Freud: Examining the Essence of his Contribution*, Basingstoke, Palgrave Macmillan.

Chapter 2 A Brief Biography (pages 6–14)

1 For a detailed and insightful account of Erikson's life, to which I am indebted as one of the sources for this account, see *Identity's Architect: A Biography of Erik H. Erikson*, by the historian Lawrence J. Friedman (London, Free Association Books, 1999).
2 E.H. Erikson (1950) *Childhood and Society,* New York, Norton. Reprinted in paperback (1977) by Triad/Paladin.
3 E.H. Erikson (1959) *Young Man Luther: a study in psychoanalysis and history,* London, Faber.
4 E.H. Erikson (1969) *Gandhi's Truth,* London, Faber.
5 E.H. Erikson (1968) *Identity: Youth and Crisis,* London, Faber.
6 E.H. Erikson (1959) *Identity and the Life Cycle,* New York, International University Press.
7 E.H. Erikson (1964) *Insight and Responsibility,* London, Faber.
8 E.H. Erikson (1975) *Life History and the Historical Moment,* New York, Norton.

9   E.H. Erikson (1977) *Toys and Reasons: stages in the ritualization of experience*, London, Marion Boyars.
10 For discussion of this issue see Chapter 9 in Richard Stevens (2008) *Sigmund Freud: Examining the Essence of his Contribution*, Basingstoke, Palgrave Macmillan.

Chapter 3 Triple Book-keeping (pages 15–42)

1   E.H. Erikson (1950) *Childhood and Society,* New York, Norton. Reprinted in paperback (1977) by Triad/Paladin, pp.31–2.
2   *Ibid.,* p.40.
3   See, for example, J. Piaget (1955) *The Construction of Reality in the Child,* London, Routledge and Kegan Paul.
4   E.H. Erikson (1950) *op. cit.*
5   *Ibid.,* p.58.
6   *Ibid.,* p.55.
7   A. Gesell (1934) *An Atlas of Infant Behaviour,* vol. 1, New Haven, Yale University Press.
8   E.H. Erikson (1950) *op. cit.,* p.62.
9   See, for example, H.R. Schaffer (1975) 'Early social behaviour and study of reciprocity', in H. Brown and R. Stevens (eds) *Social Behaviour and Experience: multiple perspectives,* London, Hodder and Stoughton/Open University Press.
10 E.H. Erikson (1950) *op. cit.,* p.60.
11 E.H. Erikson (1964) The inner and outer space: reflections on womanhood', *Daedalus 93*, pp.582–606. Revised as 'Womanhood and the inner space' in Erikson (1968) *Identity: Youth and Crisis*, London, Faber.
12 E.H. Erikson (1950) *op. cit.,* p.87.
13 *Ibid.,* p.87.
14 E.H. Erikson (1968) *Identity: Youth and Crisis,* London, Faber, p.271.
15 E.H. Erikson (1975) 'Once more the inner space', in *Life History and the Historical Moment,* New York, Norton, pp.225–47.
16 *Ibid.,* p.228.
17 *Ibid.,* p.228.
18 E.H. Erikson (1968) *op. cit.,* p.276.
19 *Ibid.,* p.284.
20 E.H. Erikson (1939) 'Observations on Sioux education', *Journal of Psychology, 7,* pp.105–56.
    E.H. Erikson (1943) *Observations on the Yurok: childhood and world image,* Monograph, University of California Publications in American Archaeology and Ethnology, 35, pp.257–301.
    E.H. Erikson (1946) 'Childhood and tradition in two American Indian tribes', in *The Psychoanalytic Study of the Child,* vol. 1, pp.319–50, Imago.
21 E.H. Erikson (1950) *op. cit.,* p.120.
22 This issue is discussed in R. Stevens (2008) *Sigmund Freud: Examining the Essence of his Contribution,* Basingstoke, Palgrave Macmillan, Chapter 10. For excellent and detailed reviews of the studies in question see P. Kline (1981) *Fact and Fantasy in Freudian Theory,* London, Methuen; or S. Fisher and R.P. Greenberg (1977) *The Scientific Credibility of Freud's Theories and Therapy,* Hassocks, Harvester Press.
23 E.H. Erikson (1950) *op. cit.,* p.120.
24 *Ibid.,* p.124.
25 *Ibid.,* p.173.
26 *Ibid.,* p.133.

27 *Ibid.*, p.164.
28 *Ibid.*, p.117.
29 *Ibid.*, p.141.
30 E.H. Erikson (1968) *op. cit.*, p.154.
31 E.H. Erikson (1950) *op. cit.*, p.171.
32 Erikson believed that the major rituals of a culture, like the Sun Dance of the Sioux, also often reflect this cycle of what he calls usurpation and atonement.
33 See B. Bettelheim (1976) *The Uses of Enchantment: the meaning and importance of fairy tales,* London, Thames and Hudson.
34 E.H. Erikson (1968) *op. cit.*, p.130.
35 E.H. Erikson (1950) *op. cit.*, p.186.
36 E.H. Erikson (1968) *op. cit.*, p.218.
37 E.H. Erikson (1950) *op. cit.*, p.199.
38 E.H. Erikson (1977) *Toys and Reasons: stages in the ritualization of experience,* London, Marion Boyars, p.44.
39 E.H. Erikson (1950) *op. cit.*, p.199.
40 S. Freud (1920) *Beyond the Pleasure Principle,* Standard Edition, (ed. J. Strachey), vol. XVIII.
41 E.H. Erikson (1950) *op. cit.*, p.190.
42 *Ibid.*, p.216.

Chapter 4 The Life Cycle (pages 43–59)

1   E.H. Erikson (1950) *Childhood and Society,* New York, Norton. Reprinted in paperback (1977) by Triad/Paladin.
2   E.H. Erikson (1959) *Identity and the Life Cycle,* New York, International Universities Press. Reprinted 1980.
3   E.H. Erikson (1964) *Insight and Responsibility,* London, Faber.
4   E.H. Erikson (1968) *Identity: Youth and Crisis,* London, Faber.
5   E.H. Erikson (1961) 'The roots of virtue', in J. Huxley (ed.) *The Humanist Frame,* London, Allen and Unwin.
6   See, for example, D.J. Levinson (1978) *The Seasons of a Man's Life,* New York, Knopf.
7   E.H. Erikson (1968) *op. cit.*, p.93.
8   *Ibid.*, p.96.
9   E.H. Erikson (1977) *Toys and Reasons: stages in the ritualization of experience,* London, Marion Boyars.
10 E.H. Erikson (1950) *op. cit.*, p.222.
11 E.H. Erikson (1964) *op. cit.*, p.118.
12 E.H. Erikson (1950) *op. cit.*, p.225.
13 E.H. Erikson (1977) *op. cit.*, p.90.
14 E.H. Erikson (1968) *op. cit.*, pp.108–9.
15 *Ibid.*, pp.109–10.
16 E.H. Erikson (1977) *op. cit.*, p.93.
17 E.H. Erikson (1964) *op. cit.*, p.119.
18 E.H. Erikson (1968) *op. cit.*, p.121.
19 E.H. Erikson (1964) *op. cit.*, p.122.
20 E.H. Erikson (1976) 'Reflections on Dr Borg's life cycle', *Daedalus, 105,* p.26.
21 E.H. Erikson (1977) *op. cit.*, p.104.
22 E.H. Erikson (1950) *op. cit.*, p.234.
23 E.H. Erikson (1976) *op. cit.*, p.25.

24 E.H. Erikson (1977) *op. cit.*, p.107.
25 *Ibid.*, p.110.
26 E.H. Erikson (1950) *op. cit.*, p.237.
27 *Ibid.*, p.237.
28 *Ibid.*, p.239.
29 E.H. Erikson (1964) *op. cit.*, p.129.
30 E.H. Erikson (1977) *op. cit.*, p.110.
31 E.H. Erikson (1950) *op. cit.*, p.240.
32 E.H. Erikson (1964) *op. cit.*, p.131.
33 E.H. Erikson (1961) *op. cit.*, p.160.
34 E.H. Erikson (1964) *op. cit.*, p.131.
35 E.H. Erikson (1977) *op. cit.*, p.111.
36 E.H. Erikson (1976) *op. cit.*, p.23.
37 E.H. Erikson (1950) *op. cit.*, p.241.
38 E.H. Erikson (1964) *op. cit.*, p.134.
39 E.H. Erikson (1950) *op. cit.*, p.242.
40 E.H. Erikson (1964) *op. cit.*, p.139.
41 C. Gilligan (1982) *In a Different Voice*, Cambridge MA, Harvard University Press.
42 See Chapter 6.
43 E.H. Erikson (1976) *op. cit.*, p.20.
44 E.H. Erikson (1950) *op. cit.*, p.243.
45 E.H. Erikson (1964) *op. cit.*, p.147.
46 E.H. Erikson (1976) *op. cit.*
47 *Ibid.*, p.24.

Chapter 5 Psychosocial Identity (pages 60–80)

1 E.H. Erikson (1950) *Childhood and Society*, New York, Norton. Reprinted in paperback (1977) by Triad/Paladin.
2 E.H. Erikson (1959a) *Identity and the Life Cycle*, New York, International Universities Press.
3 E.H. Erikson (1968) *Identity: Youth and Crisis*, London, Faber.
4 E.H. Erikson (1950) *op. cit.*, p.253. Or, rather than the different emphases being a function of changing society, was it that repression was a key feature of Freud's personality and identity the focus of personal concern for Erikson?
5 E.H. Erikson (1950) *op. cit.*, p.256.
6 E.H. Erikson (1968) *op. cit.*, p.256.
7 W. James (1920) *The Letters of William James* (ed. H. James), vol. 1, Boston, The Atlantic Monthly Press, p.199.
8 E.H. Erikson (1968) *op. cit.*, p.217.
9 *Ibid.*, p.163.
10 *Ibid.*, p.22.
11 *Ibid.*, p.156.
12 E.H. Erikson (1959a) *op. cit.*, p.109.
13 E.H. Erikson (1968) *op. cit.*, pp.22–3.
14 *Ibid.*
15 *Ibid.*, p.159.
16 *Ibid.*, p.159.
17 E.H. Erikson (1959b) *Young Man Luther: a study in psychoanalysis and history*, London, Faber, p.12.

18 E.H. Erikson (1968) *op. cit.,* pp.132–3.
19 E.H. Erikson (1975a) *Life History and the Historical Moment,* New York, Norton, pp.196–7.
20 E.H. Erikson (1959b) *op. cit.,* p.39.
21 E.H. Erikson (1968) *op. cit.,* p.175.
22 E.H. Erikson (1977) *Toys and Reasons: stages in the ritualization of experience,* London, Marion Boyars, p.122.
23 E.H. Erikson (1975b) 'Conversations with Erik Erikson'; interviews by Richard Stevens for BBC/OU radio.
24 E.H. Erikson (1968) *op. cit.,* p.169.
25 *Ibid.,* p.90.
26 *Ibid.,* p.165.
27 *Ibid.,* p.165.
28 L.J. Friedman (1999) *Identity's Architect: A Biography of Erik H. Erikson,* London, Free Association Books, pp.318–19.
29 See, for example, Erikson (1968) *op. cit.*
30 E.H. Erikson (1968) *op. cit.,* p.150.
31 G.B. Shaw (1952) *Selected Prose,* New York, Dodd, Mead.
32 E.H. Erikson (1968) *op. cit.,* p.20.
33 E.H. Erikson (1964) *Insight and Responsibility,* London, Faber, p.93.
34 E.H. Erikson (1950) *op. cit.*
35 E.H. Erikson (1977) *op. cit.*
36 E.H. Erikson (1950) *op. cit.,* p.259.
37 E.H. Erikson (1977) *op. cit.,* p.160.
38 E.H. Erikson (1942) 'Hitler's imagery and German youth', *Psychiatry,* 5, pp.475–93. Revised in C. Kluckhohn and H.A. Murray (eds) *Personality in Nature, Society and Culture,* London, Cape, pp.485–510. Also, E.H. Erikson (1950) *op. cit.,* Chapters 9 and 10.
39 E.H. Erikson (1950) *op. cit.,* p.304.
40 *Ibid.,* p.311.
41 *Ibid.,* p.320.
42 E.H. Erikson (1968) *op. cit.,* p.41.
43 *Ibid.,* pp.48–9.
44 J. Baldwin (1964) *Nobody Knows My Name. More notes of a native son,* London, Michael Joseph.
45 E. Cleaver (1969) *Soul on Ice,* London, Cape.
46 Malcolm X (1970) *Autobiography* (ed. A. Haley), Harmondsworth, Penguin.

Chapter 6 Psychobiographical Studies (pages 81–104)

1 E.H. Erikson (1954) 'The dream specimen of psychoanalysis', *Journal of American Psychoanalytic Association,* 2, pp.5–56. Revised in E.H. Erikson (1968) *Identity: Youth and Crisis,* London, Faber.
2 E.H. Erikson (1955) 'Freud's "The Origins of Psychoanalysis"', *International Journal of Psychoanalysis,* 36, pp.1–15. Here Erikson made the interesting point, later to be taken up by Bruno Bettelheim, that the translation did not always convey the essence of Freud's original meaning in German and in fact sometimes served to distort it.
3 See Chapter 2, p.12. Also E.H. Erikson (1956) 'The first psychoanalyst', *Yale Review,* 46, pp.40–62. Reprinted in E.H. Erikson (1964) *Insight and Responsibility,* London, Faber.
4 E.H. Erikson (1977) *Toys and Reasons: stages in the ritualization of experience,* London, Marion Boyars.

5   S. Freud (1910) 'Leonardo da Vinci and a memory of his childhood', *Standard Edition,*
    vol. XI, London, Hogarth Press.
6   See D.E. Stannard (1980) *Shrinking History: on Freud and the failure of psychohistory,*
    New York, Oxford University Press.
7   E.H. Erikson (1959) *Young Man Luther: a study in psychoanalysis and history,* London,
    Faber, p.191.
8   *Ibid.,* pp.44–5.
9   D.E. Stannard (1980) *op. cit.*
10 E.H. Erikson (1959) *op. cit.,* p.168.
11 *Ibid.,* p.187.
12 *Ibid.,* p.71.
13 *Ibid.,* p.163.
14 *Ibid.,* p.245.
15 *Ibid.,* p.148.
16 Several commentators assume that Luther suffered at the hands of his father: for
    example, H. Boehmer (1957) *Martin Luther: Road to Reformation*, London, Constable,
    and P. Reiter (1937) *Martin Luthers Umwelt, Charakter und Psychose*, Copenhagen,
    Leven and Munksgaard. P. Smith (1913) in 'Luther's early development in the light
    of psychoanalysis', *American Journal of Psychology,* vol. XXIV, also goes further in
    seeing this as an important factor in what he regards as Luther's Oedipus complex.
17 *Ibid.,* p.58.
18 *Ibid.,* p.241.
19 *Ibid.,* p.36.
20 *Ibid.,* p.20.
21 *Ibid.,* p.85.
22 *Ibid.,* p.159.
23 *Ibid.,* pp.249–50.
24 *Ibid.,* p.251.
25 *Ibid.,* p.255.
26 *Ibid.,* p.163.
27 *Ibid.,* p.218.
28 P. Rieff (1965) *Freud: the Mind of the Moralist,* London, Methuen.
29 E.H. Erikson (1959) *op. cit.,* p.65.
30 D.E. Stannard (1980) *op. cit.*
31 E.H. Erikson (1959) *op. cit.,* p.13.
32 F. Weinstein (1980) 'On the social function of intellectuals', in M. Albin (ed.) *New
    Directions in Psychohistory: the Adelphi papers in honor of Erik H. Erikson,* Lexington,
    Lexington Books, p.3.
33 E.H. Erikson (1959) *op. cit.,* p.47.
34 E.H. Erikson (1969) *Gandhi's Truth,* London, Faber.
35 E.H. Erikson (1968) 'On the nature of psycho-historical evidence. In search of
    Gandhi', *Daedalus, 97,* pp.695–730. Reprinted in E.H. Erikson (1975) *Life History and
    the Historical Moment,* New York, Norton.
36 M.K. Gandhi (1927) *An Autobiography or the Story of my Experiments with Truth,* trans-
    lated from the original in Gujerati by M. Dasai, Ahmedabad, Navajivan.
37 E.H. Erikson (1969) *op. cit.,* p.87.
38 E.H. Erikson (1975) *Life History and the Historical Moment,* New York, Norton, p.125.
39 *Ibid.,* p.145.
40 E.H. Erikson (1969) *op. cit.,* p.440.
41 Martin Buber had published an open letter to Gandhi in 1938 and it is very likely
    that Erikson had read this.
42 *Ibid.,* pp.230–1.
43 *Ibid.,* p.233.

44 *Ibid.,* p.251.
45 *Ibid.,* p.37.
46 *Ibid.,* p.98.
47 *Ibid.,* p.250.
48 *Ibid.,* p.99.
49 E.H. Erikson (1975) *op. cit.,* p.135.
50 *Ibid.,* p.155.
51 *Ibid.,* p.164.
52 E.H. Erikson (1969) *op. cit.,* p.405.
53 *Dharma* and *Moksha* have already been referred to earlier in the text. According to Erikson, *Artha* refers to 'the reality of family relations, of communal power and of productivity'.
54 E.H. Erikson (1969) *op. cit.,* p.42.
55 E.H. Erikson (1968) 'Freedom and Nonviolence', in E.H. Erikson (1975) *op. cit.*
56 E.H. Erikson (1969) *op. cit.,* pp.390–1.
57 *Ibid.,* p.416.
58 *Ibid.,* p.234.
59 *Ibid.,* p.251.

Chapter 7 The Nature of Erikson's Contribution (pages 105–24)

1   R.S. Wallerstein (1998) Erik H. Erikson, 1902–1994, 'Setting the Context', in R.S. Wallerstein and L. Goldberger (eds) *Ideas and Identities: The Life and Work of Erik Erikson,* Madison, International Universities Press, p.1.
2   Letter written by President Clinton to Joan Erikson, 13 May 1994.
3   R. Stevens (2008) *Sigmund Freud: Examining the Essence of his Contribution,* Basingstoke, Palgrave Macmillan.
4   E.H. Erikson (1964) *Insight and Responsibility,* London, Faber.
5   E.H. Erikson (1977) *Toys and Reasons: stages in the ritualization of experience,* London, Marion Boyars, p.117.
6   E.H. Erikson (1950) *Childhood and Society,* New York, Norton. Reprinted in paperback (1977) by Triad/Paladin, pp.201–2.
7   E.H. Erikson (1964) *op. cit.,* p.53.
8   *Ibid.,* p.71.
9   *Ibid.,* p.75.
10 E. Fromm (1941) *Escape from Freedom,* New York, Rinehart. (The subsequent British publication of the book by Routledge was retitled *Fear of Freedom.*) Friedman (1999) points out that Erikson had talked about this book at a meeting of the San Francisco Psychoanalytic Society in 1943.
11 For further discussion of the work of Fromm see Annette Thomson's book in the *Mindshapers* series: *Erich Fromm: Explorer of the Human Condition* (Basingstoke, Palgrave Macmillan, 2008).
12 Some (e.g. Friedman) have seen an influence on Erikson from the British object relations school. Certainly both approaches are people centred. But Erikson still retains a significant emphasis on instinct theory. Friedman suggests that the failure to acknowledge any connection here may also have been due to Erikson's need to avoid rejection by the Freudian school.
13 J. Marcia (1994) 'The empirical study of ego identity', in H. Bosma, T. Graafsma, H. Grotevant and D. de Levita (eds) *Identity and Development: An Interdisciplinary Approach,* London, Sage.

14   E.H. Erikson (1950) *op. cit.*, p.223.
15   E.H. Erikson (1975a) 'Conversations with Erik Erikson'; interviews by Richard Stevens for BBC/OU radio, p.6.
16   *Ibid.*, p.7.
17   E.H. Erikson (1950) *op. cit.*, p.59.
18   E.H. Erikson (1975a) *op. cit.*
19   J. Habermas (1972) *Knowledge and Human Interests,* translated by J.J. Shapiro, London, Heinemann.
20   For a fuller discussion of psychoanalysis as the study of meaning and the problems this poses, see R. Stevens (2008) *op. cit.,* Chapter 11.
21   E.H. Erikson (1968) *Identity: Youth and Crisis,* London, Faber, p.43.
22   E.H. Erikson (1970) 'Autobiographic notes on the identity crisis', *Daedalus,* Fall. Revised in E.H. Erikson (1975b) *Life History and the Historical Moment,* New York, Norton.
23   M. Berman (1975) 'Review of *Life History and the Historical Moment* by Erik Erikson', *New York Times Book Review,* 30 March.
24   E.H. Erikson (1975b) *Life History and the Historical Moment,* New York, Norton, p.29.
25   E.H. Erikson (1950) *op. cit.,* p.14.
26   Personal communication cited in R. Coles (1973) *Erik H. Erikson, the Growth of his Work,* London, Souvenir Press.
27   E.H. Erikson (1975b) *op. cit.,* p.30.
28   E.H. Erikson, personal communication in R. Coles (1973) *op. cit.,* pp.180–1.
29   M. Berman (1975) *op. cit.*
30   E.H. Erikson (1959) *Young Man Luther: a study in psychoanalysis and history,* London, Faber, p.209.
31   E.H. Erikson (1950) *op. cit.,* p.258.
32   See R. Stevens (2008) *op. cit.* for development of this theme.
33   E.H. Erikson (1950) *op. cit.,* p.375.
34   *Ibid.,* p.375.

Index

Where there are several page numbers given, bold numbers indicate a major reference to a person or concept.
Italicized numbers denote an entry in *References and Notes*.